Live Long Live Rich

Creating Your Retirement Paycheck

Live Long Live Rich

Creating Your Retirement Paycheck

By

H Craig Rappaport

Accredited Wealth
Management Advisor

First published by Dog Ear Publishing
4010 W. 86th Street, Ste H
Indianapolis, IN 46268
www.dogearpublishing.net

dog ear
PUBLISHING

ISBN: 978-159858-335-9

This book is printed on acid-free paper.

Printed in the United States of America

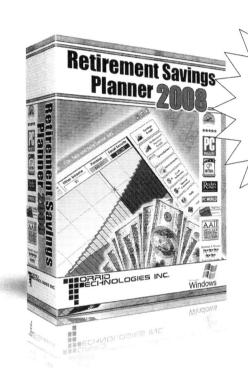

Living well is the best revenge.

George Herbert
English clergyman / metaphysical poet

I am opposed to millionaires,

but it would be dangerous to offer me the position.

Mark Twain
American author / humorist / lecturer

Dedication

To my loving wife Mindy
and my two beautiful children
Alexis and Spencer.

Preface

To paraphrase an old saying, some days you get the bear or the bull (market), and some days it gets you. The trick is to figure out how to continue generating income during your retirement years, while at the same time protecting your portfolio.

For several decades now, the baby boom generation has been preparing for retirement. Some are already there. For many wealthy investors, the accumulation phase will continue to be part of their portfolios. However, safety and income are becoming the mantra of a new breed of investors—those looking to live a vibrant, travel-filled retirement where money is a tool to fuel their passions, not something to worry about.

In my practice as an Accredited Wealth Management Advisor, my colleagues and I are hearing from a growing number of investors who want to stop risking capital and start finding ways to preserve what they have saved and to make those savings continue to grow in a way that will support the lifestyle they envision for themselves.

Unfortunately, when it comes to putting their capital to work to provide income, many investors are at a loss as to where to begin. To be sure, stores are overrun with books about investing in the stock market. Where is there a guide to help people—especially early and soon-to-be retirees—invest to create income for the twenty to thirty years most people will live after retirement? The answer is there was not one.

Until now.

For over twenty years, I have worked with investors to help them accumulate the assets necessary to fulfill their dreams. Now, after years in the "accumulation" phase of their financial lives, many of my clients are ready to move on to the next stage—to start realizing those dreams.

Live Long, Live Rich is the first guide for retirees and soon-to-be retirees who want to know how to invest to create a retirement income stream.

Using stocks, bonds, mutual funds, annuities, CDs, and a variety of conservative strategies, this book will teach you how to maintain an income stream that will help you do what everyone has worked their whole lives for: Retire in style! No worries. No sleepless nights.

It is time to take the first step toward creating your *retirement paycheck.*

Table of Contents

Illustrations

Tables

Chapter 2

Chapter 3

Chapter 6

Chapter 7

Introduction: Livin' Large

"Livin' large" is 1970s street vernacular for living well and enjoying life to the fullest. If you have not thought about exactly what you plan to do with your time after you retire, then you may not be ready to retire just yet. The thing to remember is that everything—even something as simple as visiting your grandchildren—costs.

So visualize your retirement as you are hoping it will be and as you have saved for it. What dreams do you plan to fulfill? A trip around the world? A cruise around the Greek Isles? A sailboat? A Winnebago? A seaside beach home? A summer "golf" camp to shave a few strokes off your game? Perhaps you want to turn that hobby you have enjoyed for many years into a business.

The old definition of *retirement* as simply the end of work is now, for most people, inoperable. Today, the decision to retire depends on what you want to do, when you want to do it, how long you want to keep doing it, and whether you have created sufficient retirement income to allow you the freedom to do it. The goal of this book is to help you learn how best to achieve those financial goals.

Because people are now living so much longer, retirement is a long-term proposition regardless of when you decide to do it. A sixty-five-year-old male in reasonably good health has a better-than-average chance of living to age eighty-five and a good chance of reaching ninety. A sixty-five-year-old woman has an even better than average chance of living to eighty-five and a better chance of reaching ninety. Do the math. Then ask yourself if your retirement savings will last twenty-five to thirty years after you retire?

Although the average retirement age remains sixty-five, there is ample evidence to suggest that the retirement age is rising. There are number of reasons for this, not least among them:

- The 2000–2002 bear market did considerable damage to many portfolios and served as a reality check. Many people were forced to delay retirement as a result or at the very least to scale back expectations of lifestyle after retirement.
- Reductions in pension plans. Many, if not most companies, have responded to economic pressures by cutting back (in some cases drastically) on pension plan benefits for retirees. For millions of people, this has translated into deferred and/or delayed retirement.
- Inflation has a significant impact on the value of your investments and must be considered. As a rule, inflation averages less than 4 percent a year. That means that in twenty years the same goods and services could cost you nearly twice as much as they might today. Remember, there have been (and probably will be in the future) periods during which inflation is considerably higher. Inflation is a constant fact of financial life. Inflation is the elephant in the corner of your living room. You might prefer to ignore it, but that is not possible.
- Finally yet importantly, health care—the big fat worm in the big apple of retirement.

Fact: Health care costs after retirement are likely to be higher than you think with the biggest portion going toward long-term care and prescription drugs. In general, health care costs may account for as much as one-quarter of postretirement expenses, depending on your age at retirement. That is one quarter—as in 25 percent!
If you have been retired for some time, you already know this. Bottom line? The longer you live, the more medical care you are likely to require; the more medication you are apt to need, the more it will cost you. (<u>Note:</u> If you needed a little more incentive to stop smoking, start eating a healthy diet, and get regular exercise, consider yourself incentivized!)
Then there is long-term care. Even though most older people can take care of themselves and emphatically prefer to do so for as long as possible, statistics show that one out of every ten Americans over age sixty-five will spend at least five years in assisted-living or a nursing home, or will require medical care at home. Depending on which type of care you need, the cost could run from $50,000 to $100,000 per year or more.

As seventy-seven million baby boomers are about to discover, unless you are a walking retirement whiz kid, when it comes to retirement, getting professional help can be a good idea. It should hardly be necessary to say that you should choose a financial advisor in whom you have implicit trust. Still, people often select the person to help them with financial matters based on unreliable information or without having done any real homework. This is too important a decision to be taken lightly. The best comparison, I believe, is to consider the relationship you have with your physician. Ideally, you feel comfortable sharing even the most personal information freely so that he or she can bring all available expertise to bear to keep you healthy and strong. If you hold back information from your doctor, you are hurting yourself.

In many respects, financial information is no less personal and certainly no less important. Your financial advisor must be someone with whom you feel completely comfortable sharing all information about your financial situation—and about your hopes, dreams, plans, and where you see yourself and your family in the future.

While my goal in this book is not to tout the services of one financial planner over another, I would be doing you a tremendous disservice if I failed to point out how important getting such help can be to your future. You wish to enjoy this future after you retire and wish your family to enjoy it as well.

Whether you decide to engage the services of a CFP, financial advisor, consultant, or to take the reigns of your financial future into your own hands, you will need to educate yourself about what you are facing. That is what this book is about: educating you in the fine planning and art of turning your current investments into a viable retirement income stream.

Chapter 1 covers optimal asset distribution and allocation. This is a critical element not only for enjoying your retirement comparatively free of financial worries but also for ensuring that your savings and investments continue to grow during your retirement years.

Chapter 2 gets into the nuts and bolts of retirement planning—401(k)s, the different types of IRAs, certificates of deposit (CDs), rollovers, etc. The goal here is twofold. First, we want to help you develop a retirement income stream using a variety of investment instruments and strategies to suit your personal financial situation. Second, we want to show you the most effective methods for making withdrawals when you retire and how to make that income last throughout your retirement years.

For each investment instrument, I have included a "bottom line" overall evaluation to help you determine whether a particular investment is suitable for you. In essence, this chapter is about creating your retirement paycheck.

Chapter 3 is about bonds, securities, and other investment instruments and their value as part of your retirement portfolio.

Chapter 4 covers stocks and equities, a critical component of your portfolio to sustain growth during retirement.

In chapter 5, we discuss mutual funds, which can be an invaluable tool in retirement planning and sustaining retirement income.

Chapter 6 covers annuities, i.e., one of the most successful means by which you can guarantee a steady income stream throughout your retirement years.

In chapter 7, we discuss the various investment models and strategies preferred by many financial experts and with which you should be familiar should you decide to engage the services of a financial advisor.

Chapter 8 covers the process of finding and identifying the right financial advisor or professional money manager to help you achieve the financial goals you have set for yourself during your retirement years.

Chapter 9 is a brief summary of material covered in this book.

With continued and well-crafted financial planning, retirement can be the beginning of a new life full of hope and virtually endless possibilities.

Chapter 1

ASSET ALLOCATION

This chapter is designed to help you create and maintain the best possible asset allocation in your portfolio, and to help you diversify those assets as necessary, so that your investments will continue to grow and generate income for you throughout your retirement years.

Surprisingly few new retirees or pre-retirees have a plan for the allocation of their portfolio assets. However, if your portfolio is to be a source of financial security during your retirement years, then it must be carefully tended—like a garden—so that it continues to grow. Apart from the obvious benefit of additional resources during your retirement years, there are a number of factors that reinforce the necessity for continued portfolio growth.

- Inflation erodes assets, which could make it necessary for you to lower your standard of living—not a happy thought.
- You might be forced to make withdrawals at a percentage rate that is higher than your percentage rate of earnings. This substantially shortens the life of

your portfolio. Remember, your goal is to make your assets last as long as you do—or longer.

- With medical science now making it possible for us to live longer, maintaining steady growth in your portfolio's assets takes on a completely new level of importance.
- Finally, a weakened portfolio necessarily limits what you can pass along to your heirs.

In the event that your retirement income alone will not cover your postretirement expenses, ideally the earnings from your portfolio will make up the difference. Even if you are one of those who has saved enough so that you will not have to work after you retire, your portfolio will require regular attention if it is to help support the lifestyle you wish to enjoy during retirement.

Making the Most of Your Assets

Asset allocation is part of the general retirement planning process—the goal of which is to determine the optimal allocation prior to the selection of individual assets or classes of assets. Put a different way, asset allocation establishes portfolio policy. Your funds are invested in various types of assets thus allowing you to achieve your financial goals and to take advantage of risk reduction through optimal portfolio diversification.

There are three types of asset classes: stocks (equities), bonds (fixed income), and cash (liquid assets). The percentage of each asset class in your portfolio depends on a number of variables, including but not limited to your financial goals, current savings and investment plan, time horizon, and risk tolerance. Bear in mind that *over 90 percent* of the performance of your portfolio is predicated on how the assets are allocated.

(Security selection, market timing, and other factors also affect performance but to a lesser degree.)

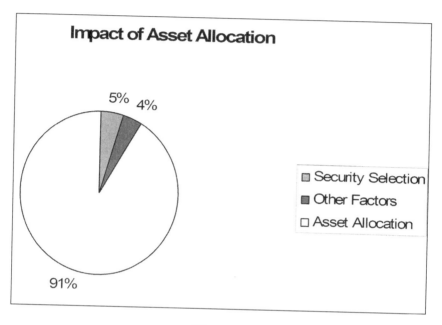

Impact of Asset Allocation

5% 4%

☐ Security Selection
■ Other Factors
☐ Asset Allocation

91%

Chart 1
Source: Live Long Live Rich

To reduce risk (and maximize return), select assets that complement each other. Bearing in mind, once again, that you are likely to live twenty-five to thirty years into retirement, keep at least a portion of your investments in stocks (equities) for long-term growth.

New retirees (or those who will be retiring soon) are often tempted to switch their portfolios into a very conservative mix. Although such a mix may protect your assets from decline, it also limits growth potential. If during your working years, you have maintained a balanced combination of stocks, bonds, and short-term investments, and if you have made periodic adjustments as needed to maintain the right mix of growth, income, and stability, you may not need to make any changes in your portfolio when you retire. As you get further into retirement, however, you will need to consider shifting to a more conservative mix.

D is for **Diversification and Defense**

Diversification is the process that is applied to allocated assets in your portfolio. In a well-balanced portfolio, income needs are met through interest and dividends, while emergency reserves are in money market or short-term bond funds. The remaining assets are invested in stocks for continued growth.

One could argue that a portfolio is just stocks, bonds, and cash. One could also argue that a pound cake is just flour, eggs, sugar, milk, and butter. In both cases, it is not the basic ingredients that matter so much, as how you mix them. Everyone has different tastes and, when it comes to portfolio diversification, different levels of risk tolerance.

Generally, a successful retirement portfolio combines capital appreciation with income and capital preservation. What you are looking for is the optimal balance of asset allocation in terms of equity, fixed income, and short-term investments. That optimal balance is determined by how much time you have until you will begin using your assets, how many years you expect to draw on those assets, your return objectives, and your level risk tolerance.

If you will not need the money for a while, or if you will be withdrawing those assets for a long period, then you may be in a position to allocate a higher percentage of your assets in stocks for long-term growth.

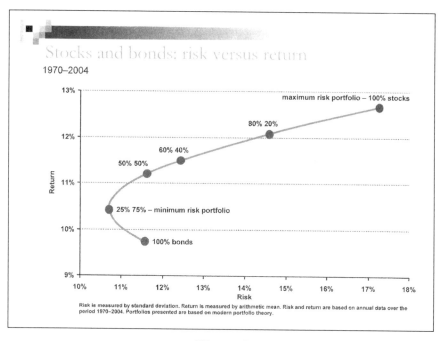

Stocks and bonds: risk versus return
1970–2004

Chart 2
Provided By: Live Long Live Rich

The above example is a simple illustration of how the addition of stocks or bonds to your portfolio affects overall risk. If you started with a portfolio of 100 percent stocks, your portfolio would settle to the far right, i.e., very high on the risk scale. As you start to add bonds to the mix, however, your risk begins to decrease, as does your overall return. Somewhere on this line is what asset allocation practitioners refer to as the *efficient frontier.* Portfolios on the efficient frontier are optimal in both the sense that they offer maximal expected return for some given level of risk and minimal risk for some given level of expected return. Without going into a more detailed explanation of that term, you need to under-stand that reducing risk does not automatically equate into an equal reduction of return. Adding an additional one, two or three asset classes can buoy returns while at the same time reducing risk.

Whatever your unique circumstance, remember that *your portfolio must continue to increase in value during your retirement years.* To protect their investments, many people, upon retirement, immediately realign portfolio assets to achieve a risk averse mixture, i.e., to minimize risk as much as possible. On the surface, this may seem like a sound move; but the reality is quite different. Not only does this realignment *decrease* the ability of our portfolio to keep pace with inflation, it also limits the growth potential that is critical to maintaining an income stream during your retirement years.

For many years, common wisdom (among financial experts) held that retirement was the time to begin moving your assets out of equities and into bonds. With the increase in life expectancy, and the tangential goal of making retirement funds last longer, that wisdom is no longer accepted as entirely correct.

Depending on how many years you would like to able to draw on your retirement savings, financial experts now suggest that you have a minimum of 50 percent (though no more than 75 percent) of your assets allocated to equities. Less than 50 percent may not support the withdrawal rate, whereas 75 percent (or more) introduces too much risk, which can also affect withdrawals.

Of course, even the savviest financial guru cannot predict how markets will perform in the future. Thus, the contents of your portfolio must be sufficiently diversified to weather financial storms.

For example, many experts suggest that your portfolio equity allocation include a percentage of international stock. Historically, the value of international stocks has held steady during times when the U.S. market was experiencing a downturn. Still, historical performance is no guarantee of future results. In addition, international stocks may be somewhat riskier due to volatility in political and economic development, regulatory differences, and differences in accounting standards. Depending on the circumstances, investment allocation in international stocks can offset other losses. Even in tough times, this is another way to maintain the optimal asset allocation balance you need to keep your portfolio growing.

In a different arena, many retirees (and pre-retirees) find commodities (i.e., oil, gas, soybeans, pork bellies, etc.) particularly attractive in part because of the excitement that seems to revolve around these types of investments. As a rule of thumb, however, retirees (or soon-to-be retirees) would do better to avoid *individual* commodity investments because of the risk and higher levels of volatility in these markets. A more prudent course would be to add commodities to one's investment portfolio through a mutual fund that is diversified over many different commodities markets. (See chapter 5 for a discussion of mutual funds.)

In the end, asset allocation is more important to the overall success of your portfolio than the specific choice of investments. At the risk of being repetitious—even though it's worth repeating—over *90 percent* of portfolio performance is usually attributable to asset allocation, *not* to individual investment choices. In Chapter 7, we will show you different ways to construct a portfolio using specific examples and generally accepted asset allocation strategies. Keep in mind how your current portfolio is allocated, and how the examples in the following chapters compare.

Chapter 2

RETIREMENT PLANS

Rollovers

In a recent television commercial, a man is shown enjoying his office retirement party at the end of which he is asked to say a few words to his friends and soon-to-be-former co-workers. "You know what I'm gonna do now?" he gleefully asks. "I'm gonna cash in my 401(k), and my wife and I are taking a trip around the world—first class all the way!" The cheers he is expecting from the crowd are not forthcoming. Instead, his announcement is met with silence and he watches, dumbfounded, while co-workers stare at him shaking their heads in a manner that clearly suggests that his plan may not be well thought out—at the least.

Over the next few years, approximately seventy-seven million baby boomers will be faced with deciding what to do with their 401(k) and other plans savings. Loosely translated, that means over $3 trillion moving through the various financial systems!

As a rule, your best bet at retirement is a *direct rollover* of your company-sponsored plan assets into a traditional

IRA. A direct rollover, i.e., transferring the balance, untouched and in one lump sum, to an IRA allows you to avoid current taxes and penalties. It also gives you access to more investment choices because IRAs allow you to buy individual investments such as CDs and stocks as well as mutual funds that may not available in standard company retirement plans.

There are some pitfalls and potential problems in the rollover process. Yet a surprisingly small percentage of people, particularly those in higher income brackets, plan to engage the services of a financial planner when they get ready to roll over their plans assets at retirement.

If you are among those who will **not** be consulting a financial planner to guide you in the rollover process, here are some tips on how to avoid costly mistakes. (**Warning: *"My dog ate the paperwork"* is generally not accepted by the IRS as an excuse.**)

- Do your homework. Tax rules governing IRAs, Roth IRAs, etc., are complicated and vary depending on what type of account you have or wish to open.
- Know the applicable deadlines. You have sixty days to move (roll over) funds from one tax-deferred account to another. Many people miss this deadline. Perhaps they sent the paperwork to the bank with instructions to "put this money into an IRA" but failed to follow up to be sure the rollover was actually completed. Perhaps you made a clerical error in filling out the necessary forms, and no one catches the error until after the sixty-day deadline has passed.
- Make copies of all paperwork, checks, and applications. Then send the original documents registered or overnight mail so that if there is a dispute, you will have records that the deposit and information was sent to the brokerage firm in a timely manner.

Although rolling over a plan into an IRA upon retirement is generally accepted as the best move, there are some exceptions.

When (and How) to Save on Taxes by __Not__ Rolling Over That 401(k)

Suppose your 401(k) retirement plan includes publicly traded company stock? You can save a great deal by paying taxes on that stock now rather than later when you take a distribution. A little known IRS regulation called *net unrealized appreciation* (NUA) allows you to pull out some (or all) of the shares in the company and separately roll the rest of your account balance over into an IRA. Any increase in the price of the stock (after you have withdrawn your shares and held them for one year) is subject only to long-term capital gains tax, which can be considerably less than ordinary income tax.

Put another way, you pay ordinary income taxes on regular IRA distributions assuming you have not yet paid taxes on contributions to the account. Normally, company stock rolled into an IRA is treated the same way. However, if instead of rolling company stock into an IRA, you withdraw the company stock from your 401(k) and transfer it to a taxable brokerage account; you bypass ordinary income taxes on the NUA of the stock. What exactly is NUA? It is the difference between the value of the company stock at the time it was purchased and put into your 401(k) and the value at the time of distribution, i.e., when it is moved out of your 401(k). Thus, your income tax, in this case, is based on the value of the stock when you first acquired it—not on the current (and presumably much higher) value.

Another advantage of the NUA tax break with regard to company stock rollover is that there is no required minimum distribution (RMD) on those assets since they are no longer a part of an IRA.

For example, if you own one thousand shares of a company stock with a current value of $100,000 with a cost basis of $25,000, you would have an NUA of $75,000. Should you liquidate the stock and withdraw it, or roll it to an IRA for eventual withdrawal, the entire amount would be subject to ordinary income tax. Assuming you are in the 30 percent tax bracket, you would owe $30,000 on the $100,000 distribution if taken in a single year.

Should you choose to adopt the NUA strategy, however, your tax bill should be much less. If you were to roll the stock, in its entirety, out of your retirement plan all at once into a personal non-IRA account, your *current* tax liability only lies with the amount you originally invested, i.e., the $25,000. Again, if you are in the 30 percent tax bracket, the current tax due would be only $7,500 ($25,000 x .30). The remaining portion, the $75,000 net unrealized appreciation, is not taxed until you liquidate it. If you hold it for more than one year, it will be taxed at the long-term capital gains rate of 15 percent. Assuming it was sold at current market value, an additional tax of $11,250 ($75,000 x 15 percent) will be due.

The tax on the $25,000 of $7,500 together with $11,250 tax equals $19,750 in total taxes. Thus, you save $10,250 by simply doing your paperwork. Not a bad way to start your retirement, don't you think?

Yes, this is a complicated concept and process. By learning about it (and getting help from a financial advisor or accountant), you are likely to save a tremendous amount. The fact is, in the circumstances described, you cannot afford **not** to take advantage of the NUA.

Caveats: This is a one-time opportunity only. So before proceeding, be certain that the parties involved understand what you are doing. If, for example, your company handles the transfer incorrectly, that could spell trouble. Also, be sure to complete both transactions—withdrawing the stock and rollover to an IRA—in the same year. Otherwise, the IRS could deny you the tax break.

Do not—I repeat, **DO NOT**—attempt to handle this type of transaction on your own. As a rule of thumb, all company stock and option transactions should be handled through a financial advisor. The dollar amounts associated with these transactions are typically large, which means that any mistakes can be quite costly. Please consult your accountant, HR person, or financial professional for some guidance before you do anything.

IRAs

With a traditional individual retirement account (IRA), taxpayers are allowed to contribute a specified maximum dollar amount for retirement savings. Depending on his or her income and coverage by other employer-sponsored retirement plan or plans, the taxpayer's contribution may be tax deductible. Withdrawals are mandatory when the taxpayer reaches age 70 1/2 and may be subject to income tax, although you are likely to be taxed at a lower rate since your income is likely to be lower in retirement. Withdrawals before the taxpayer reaches age 59 1/2 can be subject to a 10 percent penalty in addition to ordinary income tax, although there are some exceptions.

Under normal conditions, it is best to leave your IRA savings untouched until you reach 70 1/2 to take full advantage of the tax-deferred growth. There is, however, an exception to this rule. It is applicable mainly for those who are self-employed and who are likely to have the bulk of their retirement savings in one account. After you stop receiving regular paychecks, you may briefly drop into a lower tax bracket. However, you may eventually move up again once you start taking the mandatory required minimum distribution. There is a window of opportunity here. One way to ease this transition is to begin taking withdrawals earlier. Since you have temporarily dropped into a lower tax bracket, you will pay less tax on your distribution than you would have if you postponed withdrawals.

To determine how much you would need to withdraw to take advantage of the lower income tax bracket, subtract your income for the year from the highest taxable income allowed in your current income tax bracket. Then withdraw as much as you can from your IRA without bumping yourself up into a higher bracket. It could save you thousands of dollars in taxes depending on your income level. Please consult your accountant on this matter before you take a withdrawal.

Pensions

Pensions and pension plans have taken some serious blows over the past several years. Many, if not most, companies have responded to economic pressures by cutting back (in some cases drastically) on pension plan benefits for retirees.

Fewer than 25 percent of private sector workers today are covered by a company pension plan. If you are one of those who are fortunate enough to have this retirement source available to you, remember to consider your payout options carefully before making any decisions. There are four types of pension payout plans.

1. You may choose to receive your pension in the form of *a single life annuity*, i.e., a fixed amount will be paid to you each month until your death, at which point the pension benefits stop—your spouse, children, etc., <u>cannot</u> continue receiving your pension benefits.

2. You may choose to receive your pension as a joint and survivor annuity, i.e., a fixed amount is paid each month until the retiree dies, at which time a percentage of that benefit is paid to the surviving spouse until he or she dies.
3. You may choose a term certain annuity, i.e., a plan under which retirees specify that monthly payments continue for a minimum number of years, even if the retiree dies before the end of that period.
4. Finally, you may choose to receive your pension as a lump sum payment. With this option, you decide how you want to invest the money. Caution: Unless you roll the money over into an IRA, you will have to pay income taxes on the entire amount in the year you received it.

Required Minimum Distribution (RMD)

When you reach age 70 1/2, the IRS requires you to take a distribution from your retirement account whether you want to or not. The distribution must be taken by April 1 following the year in which you turn 70 1/2. After that, you must take it by December 31 in each subsequent year.

It is very easy to calculate the distribution using a table provided by the IRS. You add up your IRA balances on December 31. For instance, for the year 2006 RMD, you would take year-end 2005 IRA balances and divide by the corresponding age divisor. (See table on next page.)

IRA Distribution Calculation Table (As Used by the IRS)			
Age	Divisor	Age	Divisor
70	27.4	83	16.3
71	26.5	84	15.5
72	25.6	85	14.8
73	**24.7**	86	14.1
74	23.8	87	13.4
75	22.9	88	12.7
76	22.0	89	12.0
77	21.2	90	11.4
78	20.3	91	10.8
79	19.5	92	10.2
80	18.7	93	9.6
81	17.9	94	9.1
82	17.1	95	8.6

Chart 3
Source: IRS Uniform Distribution Table

For example, suppose I am seventy-three years old. If I had $100,000 in my IRA on December 31, 2005, the corresponding divisor would be 24.7. Dividing $100,000 by 24.7, the answer is $4,048.58—the RMD for 2006. <u>Note:</u> You must recalculate this every year.

The distribution will be taxed at ordinary income tax rates. However, it is not necessary to sell your investments to take the distribution. Instead of selling the investments, you may transfer the holding/investment to a personal account. Just make sure the total the correct overall dollar amount is equal to or above your RMD. This is called a transfer in kind. The tax would still be due but you may save on commission costs and subsequently on the reinvestment of those assets should you choose not to liquidate.

Investments Best Suited for IRAs

The old rule of thumb in saving for retirement was simple: Invest in stocks, and whatever you do, avoid capital gains (assuming your stocks showed a profit). However, the change in the tax laws has turned that investment model on its head.

An investment that pays ordinary interest, taxed at ordinary income tax levels, should be held in your IRA. Why? Because you will have to pay ordinary income tax on it eventually when you take your IRA withdrawal. Thus, there is nothing to be gained or lost by holding this type of investment in your IRA.

Conversely, investments that pay qualified dividends or that may generate capital gains that are taxed at 15 percent should be held in your personal accounts. Why? Because you pay only 15 percent on the investment by holding it in your personal, taxable account, whereas you pay ordinary income tax on the same investment when it is eventually withdrawn from your IRA.

Now, do not run out and start changing your portfolio around all at once. But as you make decisions, over time, just keep these things in mind so that when the time comes for you to decide what to do about your IRA, 401(k), etc., you can start immediately to redeploy these assets in the way that will be most profitable to you in the long term.

Conclusion

Rolling over your 401(k), 403(b), or other company retirement plan is the first step in getting your accounts ready to be invested properly for a long and rewarding retirement. If you have company stock in your plan, make sure you consult a financial professional to see if you can benefit from tak-

ing a distribution of the stock and capitalizing on the net unrealized appreciation that has hopefully occurred.

Although it is usually beneficial to leave your assets in your IRA until you are required to withdraw the minimum amount at age 70 1/2, you may be able to take advantage of the lower tax bracket. If you have a year in which your income is quite low, you can withdraw some money earlier and pay a lower income tax on the distribution.

These concepts and transactions are, by themselves, manageable. However, there are a lot of moving parts so make sure you get help and consult your financial advisors before transferring or executing a transaction that you will not be able to reverse.

Chapter 3

BONDS AND SECURITIES

For most investors, bonds are a primary way to receive income. Bonds are relatively easy to understand and the basic concept is one most investors can quickly grasp. Just in case you are unfamiliar with bonds and securities, we will take a few minutes to go over the basics so that when we move on to explaining the different types of bonds, along with their risks and reward characteristics, you will be better equipped to make a decision on what type of bonds are best for you.

A bond is a debt security. By buying bonds, you are lending money to the issuing organization (government, municipality, corporation, etc.). In return, the issuer promises to pay you a specific interest rate during the life of the bond and to pay you the principal amount at maturity. Thus, a bond works similar to a CD.

Bonds values have historically been more stable than stocks, but the trade-off for that stability has been lower returns. Most bond investors favor a predictable stream of income and stability of principal over a higher overall total return.

In addition to discussing the various types of bonds, this discussion will also cover buying the right bond at the right time. We will not focus on trading bonds for profit since the majority of retirees are unlikely to engage in those types of transactions.

A bond is a loan that must be repaid. It is this promise of principal repayment that keeps bond prices relatively stable compared to stock prices. Even if an issuer is forced into bankruptcy, bondholders are usually paid off before stock-holders in the event of liquidation.

There are a few terms and concepts you need to under-stand to compare the different bond options.

Bonds are usually issued in $1,000 or $5,000 increments. This is the *par amount*, i.e., the amount that will be returned to the investor at maturity or upon redemption. Many advisors suggest buying a minimum of $10,000. If, for some reason, you need to sell a bond, larger amounts are typically more liq-uid and may bring a higher price than small amounts.

The bond issuer promises to pay a stated annual interest rate periodically and the principal amount at maturity. For many investors, the interest rate is the first thing they con-sider. The higher the rate the better, right? Not so fast.

That old saying "You never get something for nothing" is particularly true on Wall Street. If you are being offered a higher rate than is available on a similar maturity U.S. Trea-sury bond, there is always additional risk to be considered. That does not mean the risks aren't worth it. It simply means you had better understand those risks before you buy. Finding out later may be too late.

Credit Risk

Credit quality is particularly important since it is an indi-cation of the stability of the issuing organization. For exam-ple, U.S. Treasury bonds are backed by the full faith and credit of the United States Government and are considered the safest bonds one can purchase. Although U.S. Treasury bonds carry no rating, a AAA rating is implied. One or more of the following credit rating agencies rate most other bonds. The table below lists the three primary rating agencies along with basic descriptions of each rating category.

Primary Bond Rating Agencies and Rating Categories			
Credit Risk	Moodys	S&P	Fitch
Investment Grade			
Highest Quality	Aaa	AAA	AAA
High Quality Very Strong	Aa	AA	AA
Upper Medium Grade Strong	A	A	A
Medium Grade	Baa	BBB	BBB
Not Investment Grade			
Somewhat Speculative	Ba	BB	BB
Speculative	B	B	B
Highly Speculative	Caa	CCC	CCC
Imminent Default	C	C	C
Default	C	D	D

Chart 4
Source: Investinginbonds.com

The lower the credit rating, the higher the credit risk and, ergo, the higher the chance that the bond issuer will default on the obligations. One or more of these agencies assign ratings after an in-depth analysis of the issuing organization. An analyst may assign a plus or minus to a rating, to further clarify what he or she believes to be the underlying fundamentals. Using S&P ratings, bonds rated BBB- or higher are considered investment grade and therefore appropriate for individual investors. Ratings of BB+ or lower are considered *high-yield* or *junk bonds*, which are considered below investment grade. Most investors should avoid speculative individual bonds that carry below investment grade ratings. In most cases, it is just not worth the risk.

Should you come across a bond investment opportunity where, after ***very careful consideration*** (and consultation with a financial advisor), you believe you would be justified in taking on more risk, remember that you deserve to be compensated and should receive a higher rate of interest. With more risk, you may earn more in returns, however, you take a greater chance of losing part (or all) of your principal. It is all about risk versus reward. So ask yourself, is this a risk I really should take, and am I being adequately compensated for taking that risk?

As with all types of investments, your first step is to do your homework. With bonds, the credit rating companies do some of the homework for you. Take those credit ratings to heart.

Bottom Line: Risk is a relative thing. If you need to take more risk to generate the amount of income desired, then more risk may be in order. Just make sure you are being compensated appropriately. As a rule, most investors should avoid bonds that are not investment grade. Stick to AA and AAA rated bonds to keep safety and risk in check.

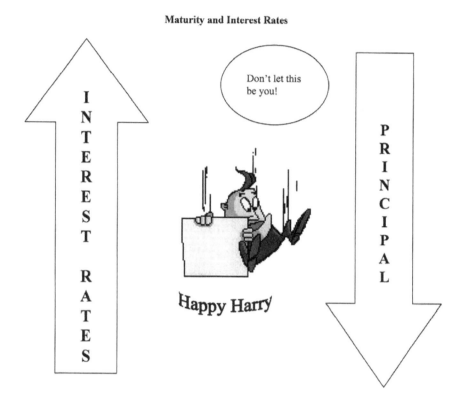

Chart 5
Maturity and Interest Rates

Maturity is the date on which the principal amount is repaid and the issuing organization returns your investment to you. You can buy bonds with maturities as short as one week or as long as one hundred years. Clearly, the maturity (or maturities) you select should be aligned with your investment objectives.

As a rule, most investors should consider bonds with maturities of 20 years or fewer. Many investors stagger the maturities of the various bonds in a portfolio to create a "ladder structure." (More about this in chapter 7.)

If you hold a bond to maturity, you will get back your initial investment. Between now and then, as interest rates fluctuate, bond prices may also fluctuate, which could have an impact on the current value of your portfolio.

Fact: If interest rates rise, the value of a bond, i.e., its *current* price, drops. If interest rates drop, the value of the bond will tend to rise. (Remember Happy Harry!) It also true that certain redemption features can inhibit price increases and decreases on a particular bond. This is a matter of math and has very little to do with the type of bond, your financial advisor, or your investment ability.

The price of a short-term bond will tend to fluctuate less than that of a long-term bond because the shorter the maturity, the sooner you will receive your principal back and the sooner you can reinvest at the going rate. Because there is less risk of price volatility with a short-term bond compared to a long-term bond, the interest rate of a short-term bond will tend to be lower. Therefore, you will earn less as risk decreases—yet *another* rule of thumb that you should keep in mind.

Okay. Time for a pop quiz.

What length of maturity would you purchase during a time of rising interest rates to avoid a decline in your current principal value?

    A.   Long
    B.   Short

The answer is B. Shorter term maturities perform better when interest rates are rising. Longer-term maturities tend to perform better when interest rates are falling. (Just ask Happy Harry!)

You may be wondering why you just would not sell the long-term bond when rates start to increase and buy a short-term bond instead. While it is, true that many nimble traders buy and sell bonds on a daily basis betting on the fluctuation of interest rates. For most investors, markets move to quickly to take advantage of such changes. Even though it is hard to know the future direction and timing of interest rates, you do need to make some sort of determination when considering your investments. Taking a long-term perspective may provide you with a more stable portfolio but certainly a more stable emotional state of mind. Remember also that the credit ratings of the issuing organization along with current trends in interest rates are two major issues to be considered if you are thinking of a bond investment.

Call Provisions

When buying a bond you will know the maturity date, but most bonds today also have *call provisions*. This means that the issuing organization has the right to redeem, call away (give your money back), earlier than the stated maturity date. An organization is most likely to do this if they can turn around and borrow again at a lower rate. (This is similar to refinancing your home to capture a lower mortgage rate.) Make sure you understand the call provisions when you purchase a bond. If interest rates are rising, the chances of the bond being called away are reduced. After all, who would refinance at a higher rate? If rates are declining, however, the chances are better that the bond would be called away. When interest rates are lower, everyone wants to refinance, even companies and governments.

So before buying a bond of any kind, make sure to ask if there is a call provision. If there is, make sure you ask for the **yield to maturity**, **yield to call**, and any other redemption features that could affect your return on the bond.

Yield to Maturity (YTM)

When you purchase a bond, the price you pay may be more or less than the maturity value. The bonds' current price will fluctuate; and on the date of purchase, it could be trading above the par value (which would make it a ***premium bond***) or below the par value (which would make it a ***discount bond.***) The premium or discount you pay affects the overall return on the investment.

If you paid $950 for a $1,000 bond, you purchased the bond at a discount, on sale so to speak. Thus, the appreciation from $950 to the maturity value of $1,000—plus the coupon—should be taken into account when evaluating the overall total return on the bond.

The same holds true for a premium bond. If you paid $1,050 for a $1,000 bond, you paid a premium. The difference between what you paid over the final maturity value would need to be subtracted to determine your overall total return.

YTM is calculated using a complicated formula that includes the present value of the principal and interest streams. Although there are other variables to consider including, but not limited to, the call provisions, the yield to maturity is a reasonable way to compare the value of bonds. Fortunately, you do not have to figure the yield yourself. It is figured out for you prior to purchase by the organization where you are purchasing them. It is easy to find out, just ask.

Yield to Call (YTC)

The YTC is determined the same way as the YTM except the call dates are used instead of the maturity date. This is particularly important if you have paid a premium for the bond since that premium is discounted over a shorter length of time and has a more negative impact. Fortunately, just as with YTM, the YTC is readily available. All you have to do is ask.

Bottom Line: Although YTM is a good starting point when evaluating a bond investment, it is also important to know the YTC. If both are satisfactory, then it may be an appropriate investment. Be aware also that investing in

premium or discount bonds may have tax implications, which should also be considered before making a purchase.

Below and on the following pages I have compiled a list of the most common fixed-income choices, along with general characterization of risk for each. Note: This information is by no means cast in stone. Credit ratings, interest rates, call features, and economic conditions at the time you are considering a purchase—all affect each bond differently.

Treasury Notes, Bills, and Bonds

Due, for the most part, to the simplicity and huge volume of outstanding issues, U.S Treasury bills, notes, and bonds are among the most liquid securities available. The credit quality is excellent since the principal and interest payments on these securities are "full faith and credit" obligations of the U.S. government. The interest is subject to federal taxation, but that interest is exempt from state and local income taxes.

Cash management bills have the shortest maturities—as little as a few days. Treasury Bills (or T-bills) are issued regularly with four-, thirteen-, and twenty-six-week maturities. T-bills and cash management bills are issued at a discount price to par value with no stated interest rate. The amount you earn is the difference between the purchase price and the maturity value.

The Treasury also issues two-, three-, five-, and ten-year notes. These bonds have a stated coupon rate and pay interest semiannually.

Treasury Inflation-Protected Securities (TIPS)

TIPS, also issued by the Treasury, usually have five-, ten-, and twenty-year maturities. The appeal of these securities is the inflation protection provided through adjustments to the amount to be paid at maturity. These adjustments are based on the Consumer Price Index for Urban Consumers (CPI-U). The maturity value rises when the CPI-U rises and falls when the CPI-U falls. These bonds generally pay less interest than other bonds with the difference to be made up in adjusting final maturity value higher.

Investors willing to accept a lower current income stream and are looking for a hedge against inflation, may be attracted to the TIPS market. Those looking solely for income should be able to find a better choice elsewhere.

Bottom Line: **U.S. Treasury bonds (of all types) are safe and secure although they are subject to price fluctuations prior to maturity. Treasury bonds are excellent vehicles for long-range planning due to the wide variety of options and maturities that can be used to fill voids in your portfolio. Because they are so safe, Treasury bonds pay a very low rate of interest compared to what may be available with other bond alternatives. Retirees who are primarily interested in income are likely to do better looking elsewhere.**

Certificates of Deposit (CDs)

CDs are time deposits, i.e., you agree to put your funds on deposit with a bank for a stated period of time, during which your funds earn interest at an agreed upon rate. In general, the longer you are willing to leave your money in a CD, the higher the rate of interest you will receive.

CDs purchased directly from banks are secured by the Federal Deposit Insurance Corporation (FDIC) in amounts up to $100,000 per investor, $250,000 for retirement accounts. CDs typically pay a stated interest rate until maturity. An investor wishing to withdraw the deposit before maturity will usually be subject to a penalty.

Brokered CDs

These are CD's purchased through your advisor at the investment firm you deal with. Most firms use many different banks so comparing interest rates is easy. These are similar to regular CDs in that they are issued directly by banks and carry FDIC insurance, and are available in a variety of maturities. Brokered CDs can be bought and sold prior to maturity, which makes them more liquid. <u>Note:</u> The price will fluctuate and may be more or less than what you paid or the maturity value if you sell them early.

Another benefit to brokered CDs is that they usually include a "survivor's option" that provides for redemption of the CD at the maturity value upon the death of the owner, even if death occurs well before maturity. *This can be an important estate-planning tool especially for an older individual who wishes to capture the higher rates associated with longer term CDs while at the same time not tying up money for his/her heirs in their estate.* Most of my older clients love this structure.

<u>Bottom Line:</u> Brokered CDs are an easy way to shop around for the best interest rates and do all your purchasing in one place even if you are buying from one institution. This will also give you an opportunity to compare current CD rates with other investments by simply asking your financial advisor to suggest other alternatives.

Step-Up CDs

Step-up CDs feature interest rates that increase (or "step up") to a predetermined level on a specific time schedule as they approach maturity. The interest rate on these CDs is usually fixed for a period of time, which is followed by a step up to another fixed rate. These steps may occur more than once before a CD reaches maturity. Let us look at an example:

Consider a ten-year CD. The first two years, it pays a 4 percent interest rate. The next two, a five percent interest rate, the next two, a six percent interest rate, and so on.

Years 1 and 2	4%
Years 3 and 4	5%
Years 5 and 6	6%
Years 7 and 8	7%
Years 9 and 10	8%

This structure usually pays a higher rate than on a short-term security and steps up at a moderate rate as the CD moves toward maturity. The downside here is that most of these issues are callable on the date of the first step-up. At that point, if the bank does not want to pay the higher stepped-up rate, it can call the CD away.

Like brokered CDs, the step-up CD usually carries a survivor's option. Again, this option makes this a great choice for older investors looking to boost their income

I have clients who would never, in their golden years, select a long-term fixed-income investment. Others are inclined to say, "Let me enjoy my money now and let my heirs worry about the inheritance and what to do with it."

This investment choice works for both types of investors.

Bottom Line: Step-up CDs are FDIC insured and, because of the various structures and maturities, should be considered by many investors, depending on their goals of course. The survivor's option makes step-ups particularly attractive for older investors, and I urge most of my clients who are senior citizens to consider adding these to their portfolio.

Corporate Bonds

As the name implies, corporate bonds are issued by private or public companies that use the funds collected for capital expenditures, project financing, and in many cases the financing of mergers and acquisitions. When you buy a corporate bond, the company promises to pay periodic interest and to return your money on a specified maturity date. <u>Note:</u> Unlike stocks, corporate bonds do not give you an ownership right in the company.

The corporate bond market is big, and investors are attracted to it for a number of reasons, including

- Diversity. You can choose from a variety of sectors, structures, and credit quality characteristics depending on your objectives.
- Safety. Corporate bonds are evaluated and rated based on credit history and repayment of obligations along with a company's financial results.
- Dependable income. Corporate bonds provide a steady stream of income while preserving the principal.
- Attractive yields. Corporate bonds usually provide higher yields than U.S. Treasury securities because, more often than not, they carry more credit risk.

Remember that the interest received from corporate bonds is subject to federal and state income tax. In addition, if you sell a corporate bond before maturity, you may be subject to a capital gain or loss as well.

<u>Bottom Line:</u> Corporate bonds are an attractive investment due to the predictability of income and the wide variety of maturities and choices. That said, however, when purchasing individual corporate bonds, investors should stay in the upper end of investment grade to minimize default risk. Do not reach for the highest yield in the sector. An abnormally high rate of return on a corporate bond is usually a sign of trouble. Remember: Wall Street never—I repeat, NEVER—give something away for

nothing. Savvy investors will compare the same maturity to a less risky option, e.g., a CD, to make sure they will be receiving an appropriately higher rate of interest for the additional risk. You will be surprised at how often the lower risk investment comes close to matching the return of a riskier option.

High-Yield Bonds

An organization that does not qualify for an investment grade rating from one of the leading agencies may issue high-yield bonds, also known as *junk bonds*. Bonds that are initially rated as investment grade may suffer a deterioration of credit quality and associated ratings so that they become high-yield investments. Although high-yield securities usually take the form of corporate bonds, they are also available as municipal bonds.

Individual high-yield securities ***are not*** appropriate for most older, individual investors. An understanding of the underlying risk and the ability and willingness to lose most or all of one's investment are essential for consideration of junk bonds. Less risk-averse investors consider diversification to be the most important part of a high-yield investment strategy.

Bottom Line: Individuals who are seeking the high yields provided by junk bonds should consider high-yield mutual funds as an alternative. Although they carry the risks associated with individual high-yield bonds, they feature professional management and diversification. In any case, these are risky investments and most retires should proceed with caution.

Asset-Backed Securities (ABS)

Asset-backed securities are bonds or notes backed by financial assets consisting mostly of first mortgages with home-equity loans, credit card loans, auto loans, and student loans making up 80 percent of the outstanding issues. (We will cover mortgage-backed and non-mortgage-backed securities later.)

From a credit quality standpoint, ABS are one of the most secure investment vehicles. They are secured by collateral to ensure that the obligations are met. Ninety percent of ABS issues have an outstanding (i.e., triple A) rating. Financial institutions that turn these loans into marketable securities create ABS. Those securities are then sold to investors who are attracted by the reduced risk, predictable cash flow, attractive yields, high credit quality, and diversity of ABS in terms of yields, structures, maturities, and collateral.

ABS offer higher yields than comparable maturity U.S. Treasury securities. ABS yields are more similar to those offered by corporate bonds of comparable maturity and credit ratings.

As with all fixed-income securities, the price of ABS fluctuates in response to interest rates and economic conditions, both of which can have negative effect on ABS prices.

Bottom Line: **ABS are an excellent source of income and should be considered by most investors. Although investing in ABS securities requires a slightly higher level of sophistication, most investors (perhaps with some professional help) should be able to understand the differences between bonds within the different ABS classes.**

Fixed-Rate Capital Securities (The New Preferred Stock)

Developed in the 1990s, fixed-rate capital securities were designed to meet the needs of income-oriented investors while creating a source of cost-efficient capital for issuers. Investors are attracted by the

- Generally higher yields,
- Fixed (i.e., monthly, quarterly, or semiannual) income,

- Predictable investment time frames,
- Defined maturity,
- Investment-grade credit quality, and
- Liquidity.

These securities, which carry names like QUIPS, TOPRS, QUIDS, QUICS, MIPS, and MIDS, among others, essentially replaced the standard preferred stocks with which most of us are familiar.

Since the safety of a fixed-rate capital security depends largely on the issuer's credit quality and ability to meet its financial obligations, any change in either of these factors can have a deleterious effect on your investment. The same care that you would take in investing in a corporate bond should be used here. As with any preferred type of security, look at these as a long-term bond, since most have final maturities of forty years. Also, remember: A rise in interest rates will have a significant effect on the value of your investment, and only a future decline in interest rates or an early call will enable you to recoup the loss.

As is the case with bonds and preferred stock, if fixed-rate capital securities are sold or otherwise disposed of before maturity, the investor may realize a capital gain or loss.

Many investors own these types of securities and generally lump them into the overall preferred stock category, which for most investors is fine.

Bottom Line: Fixed-rate capital securities are an excellent source of income and should be used by most investors looking to boost the yield on their overall portfolio. Be wary of reaching for yield in this sector during a time of rising interest rates, as the prices will drop in that event. (Remember Happy Harry)

Mortgage-Backed Securities (MBS)

These bonds are created to finance a borrower's purchase of a home or other real estate. Once these loans are made, the mortgage lenders either pool a group of mortgages together or sell the loans to another issuer. The resulting pooled securities are collectively called *mortgage-backed securities* or MBS.

MBS represent a direct ownership interest in a pool of mortgage loans. As the homeowners make mortgage payments, those payments are passed through to the MBS holder.

Most mortgage pass through securities are guaranteed by the Government National Mortgage Association (GNMA) also known as Ginnie Mae or U.S. government-sponsored entities such as the Federal National Mortgage Association (FNMA) also known as Fannie Mae or the Federal Home Loan Mortgage Corporation (FHLMC) also known as Freddie Mac. In general, these are all lumped into one category— called *agency securities.*

GNMA, FNMA, and FHLMC all guarantee the timely payment of principal and interest even if the borrowers fail to make their payments as well as the final payment of principal. Note, however, that *only* the GNMA is backed by the full faith and credit of the U.S. government. The FNMA and FHLMC are sponsored—not guaranteed. That said, however, the market views these securities as AAA rated and, thus, very secure.

Private institutions may also issue MBS that may be backed by different types of collateral such as letters of credit or specialized mortgage loan pools. Although not sponsored by a government agency, these securities are rated and often receive the AAA rating.

MBS differ from corporate or treasury bonds in a number of ways. MBS payments consist of mortgage payments that are made up of interest and principal payments. In each monthly payment, the MBS holder may receive back a piece of the original principal instead of a single lump sum payment at maturity.

In times when there is a lot of refinancing, the MBS holder may receive a lot of their principal back *before* the stated maturity date. Because this happens often, MBS are quoted on an average life basis, i.e., the average time it takes to get your principal back. This average-life time frame fluctuates with interest rates. You may receive your principal back sooner during a time when interest rates are lower. Conversely, the average life may extend during a time of rising interest rates. These risks are often quantified and spelled out clearly and available before you purchase a bond. Know, however, that there are many different series of bonds and each may carry different prepayment risk characteristics. Because of the uncertain return of principal time frame, MBS often pay higher interest than comparable Treasury bonds with similar maturities.

<u>Bottom Line</u>: As a rule, MBS are an excellent steady source of income. Investors should remember, however, that principal payment time frames are not always locked in. It is therefore wise to invest in MBS along with other more predictable bonds as part of a well-diversified portfolio.

Since different series of debt are available with different prepayment and interest rate risks, before making a purchase, investors should assess how changes in the financial environment may affect the particular bond being considered. Most of the risks can be identified with a little investigation.

Municipal Bonds (Tax Exempt)

States, cities, counties, and/or other government organizations issue tax-exempt municipal bonds usually to raise money for schools, highways, hospitals, or other civic projects.

Investors are often attracted to tax-exempt municipal bonds because the interest these bonds pay is free from federal taxes. If you buy a municipal bond in the state where you live, the interest earned may also be free of state and local taxes. Since there is no tax on the income, these bonds generally pay a lower stated interest rate than taxable bonds. If you are in a higher income bracket, tax-free municipal bonds may be the best choice for most of your bond portfolio.

How do you know if the lower tax-free yield on a municipal bond is better for you than a higher taxable yield? Well, you need to do some calculations as the table below indicates.

Tax-Exempt Yields	25% Tax Bracket	28% Tax Bracket	33% Tax Bracket	35% Tax Bracket
1%	1.33%	1.39%	1.49%	1.54
1.5	2.00	2.08	2.24	2.31
2	2.67	2.78	2.99	3.08
2.5	3.33	3.47	3.73	3.85
3	4.00	4.17	4.48	4.62
3.5	4.67	4.86	5.22	5.38
4	5.33	5.56	5.97	6.15
4.5	6.00	6.25	6.72	6.92
5	6.67	6.94	7.46	7.69
5.5	7.33	7.64	8.21	8.46
6	8.00	8.33	8.96	9.23
6.5	8.67	9.03	9.70	10.00
7	9.22	9.72	10.45	10.77

Chart 6
Source: Investinginbonds.com

Using the above chart lets look at a quick example. If the tax-exempt yield is 4 percent and I am in the 33 percent tax bracket, then I would need to earn a 5.97 percent or better on a taxable bond so that after I pay the tax, I have at least the same money in my pocket as I would have if I purchased the tax-free bond. Now you can compare the after-tax yield on each investment to see which option is best for you. Additionally, in turning your income from taxable to tax free, you may be able to reduce your overall income tax bracket—a major plus.

Tax-exempt municipal bonds can provide a predictable stream of income while giving the investor a range of options in terms of type of bond, geographical location, maturity, etc. The price fluctuations in these securities will be affected by interest rates just as with other fixed-income securities. Thus, the direction of interest rates should be considered when determining how long of a maturity to buy.

Municipal bonds have an excellent track record in terms of safety. The rating agencies rank them just like other taxable bonds. Individual investors should stay in the higher end of safety ratings, i.e., A, AA or AAA. Finally, tax-exempt municipal bonds are usually marketable should you have to sell before maturity. Note: Not all municipal bonds are exempt from federal and state taxes. So do your homework before making a purchase.

Insured Municipal Bonds

Tax-exempt municipal bonds are considered relatively safe. Conservative investors in particular may be attracted by the additional insurance under which municipal bond insurers guarantee scheduled interest payments and principal. This insurance protects the investor from default should the state or municipality fail to pay interest and return the principal at maturity. Insured municipal bonds are most often rated AAA—the highest safety rating.

Bottom Line: As a rule of thumb, those investors in the higher tax brackets who wish to take advantage of tax-free municipal interest payments purchase municipal bonds. AAA-rated insured municipal bonds should be the anchor of any bond portfolio for an investor in the upper income tax brackets.

Unit Investment Trust (UIT) (Fixed Income)

A unit investment trust (UIT) is a registered investment fund company with a fixed portfolio of income-producing securities purchased by the fund company and held to maturity. The fixed-income UIT portfolio generally consists of a basket of individual bonds. Investors buy units in the trust and receive a share of dividends or interest. Profits are passed along to the investors rather than being reinvested in the fund company. Think of the UIT as a mutual fund without management. Once the securities are selected, they are held to maturity.

By purchasing a portfolio of bonds, UITs diversify their holdings to a level that most individual investors would find impossible to achieve. For investors, this means reduced risk.

One of the major attractions of UITs is that investors receive regular income. Investors in fixed-income UITs receive income monthly.

Investors may also be attracted to UITs because as investments they are comparatively affordable and easy to purchase. An investor can buy a UIT portfolio of bonds in one transaction and at one purchase price. Because UITs offer a fixed portfolio, there are no management fees; and since buying and selling of securities is limited, transaction costs are low.

Investors should also be aware that UITs are subject to SEC oversight and are strictly regulated by federal law. Every UIT must provide investors a prospectus that includes information on the trust, its investment objectives, portfolio holdings, expenses, and terms for buying and selling units.

There are a variety of UITs that investors may find attractive, depending on their investment objectives. Investors that are more conservative may be interested in U.S. Government Securities UITs, which hold a variety of government securities including Treasury bonds and other government notes. The income from these investments is comparatively steady and the risk is minimal.

Many buy tax-free unit trusts, which are portfolios of municipal bonds that may be free of federal, state, and local taxes.

Investors who want to get into foreign fixed-income markets may wish to consider international bond units, which hold debt issues of foreign companies and governments. These units are subject to price and performance fluctuations because trusts are in foreign currencies and then converted into U.S. dollars. As investments, international bond units are somewhat riskier, though there is a higher return potential.

Investors who want to know more about the various units and the risks and potential returns would be wise to consult a financial advisor before making any final decisions. Units come in all shapes and sizes, and there are many, many choices.

Bottom Line: UITs are an excellent source of income as well as a means of achieving immediate portfolio diversification while enjoying a predictable income stream. Because there are many types of UITs available for purchase, they can be used by a wide range of investors with different risk profiles and goals. UITs are a very popular investment choice.

Conclusion

If you are retired or about to enter retirement, it is likely that a large portion of your portfolio will be invested in bonds. The bond sector is huge consisting of a variety of structures that can be somewhat difficult to understand. The general rule of thumb is to diversify among structures and sectors to achieve a balance between risk and reward.

You can build a portfolio of individual bonds, but make sure you keep risk in check by staying in the upper end of investment grade, i.e., A, AA, AAA ratings. The direction of interest rates will have a bearing on what to invest in and when.

If you are even slightly unsure about which bonds are best for you, consult a financial planner or advisor.

Chapter 4

EQUITIES

Stocks and Equity Investing

Among well-informed investors, "Buy low. Sell high" is as much of a truism as "Measure twice. Cut once" is among carpenters. As a recent retiree (or if you are about to retire), you may have shifted a small percentage of the assets in your portfolio out of stocks into lower risk investments. Depending on your situation, that may have been a wise move. In general, however, stocks should remain a large part of your portfolio.

Equities are your best choice for long-term growth and will act as a hedge against inflation and protect your purchasing power. The percentage of equities in your portfolio depends on how much risk you are willing to take, how soon you plan to start withdrawing from your portfolio, and how many years you expect that retirement income to last.

Of course, there are stocks and then there are…well… other stocks. Ideally, your portfolio will include so-called large cap stocks (i.e., shares of old-line established companies) as well as "mid-caps" (i.e., shares of medium-sized companies) and "small caps" (i.e., shares of smaller, newer companies.) along with international investments.

There are certain groups of stocks that generally pay larger dividends than others do, and we will try to point you in that direction. It is, however, more difficult to generalize about risks and dividends when it come to individual stocks as compared to other asset classes (e.g., bonds) because things can change rapidly for a particular company or market sector. In other words, a specific recommendation today may not be operable six months from now.

We will begin with some general information on equities and stocks, and then move on to a more detailed breakdown.

Dividends

Since the change in tax laws, dividends have taken on a completely new level of importance. Dividends are taxed at the 15 percent tax bracket—clearly an advantage over interest earnings, which are taxed at ordinary income tax rates. Dividends are generally paid quarterly and companies usually will make every effort to ensure that dividend payments are not interrupted. Curtailed or even reduced dividends from a company send a bad message to Wall Street.

In general, shareholders in the more mature and consistently profitable companies can expect regular dividends. In addition, certain sectors pay larger portions of their earnings in dividends to shareholders than others.

Potential investors should consider evaluating a company's dividend payout practice to determine whether the earnings are sufficient to cover the dividends paid. For this type of somewhat complicated evaluation, you would examine the company's dividend payout ratio, which gives the percentage of earnings a company is paying out in dividends. Put simply, the lower the number the better, as a lower number leaves more room for dividend growth. A company with a high dividend payout ratio will have more trouble raising pay-out rates. Moreover, should the company run into trouble, it would have less room to maneuver, which will put dividends in jeopardy.

A consistent history of increasing dividends is reassuring as well as a sign of disciplined decision making on the part of company management. Moreover, and to the extent possible, *everything* in which you invest should pay dividends. Rule of thumb: Choose an investment that will provide some income over an investment that is offering just growth.

Bottom Line: Dividends are often evidence of a company's profitability and solid management. By looking for companies that pay dividends, you not only increase your cash flow, but you also increase the stability of your individual equity portfolio.

Categories of Equities

Large Cap, Mid Cap, and Small Cap

Large cap stocks are holdings in companies with a market capitalization of over $10 billion dollars. Generally, these are the old-line companies whose names have become household words, e.g., IBM, General Electric, etc.

Mid-cap stocks are holdings in companies with a market capitalization of between $5 billion to $10 billion. Small caps are holdings in companies with market a capitalization below $5 billion.

Buying individual stocks increases your risk as compared to other more diversified investments. If you are buying stock in mid- or small-cap companies, the risk rises exponentially. It should be noted, however, that these defini-

tions (large cap, mid cap, small cap) often vary from one brokerage house to another. In fact, these definitions are just
approximations that can, and often do, change over time.

Small caps sometimes get short shrift from investors.
Their very name—*small* caps—reduces their appeal especially when compared to the big kids on the block. However,
investors who overlook small caps are making a mistake.
Downplaying small caps can lead to significant missed investment opportunities. That said, however, keeping in mind that
small caps are harder to research and are often more volatile,
a mutual fund or index is probably the best venue for purchase
rather than buying individual small cap stocks.

**Bottom Line: If you are inclined to purchase individ-
ual securities, sticking to large caps will probably let you
sleep better at night. On the other hand, well-informed
investors know that large caps represent only a small portion of publicly traded stocks. Those stocks among the
smaller classifications warrant equal attention. Thus, the
well-diversified portfolio includes a balance of large, mid-
, and small cap stocks. Buying individual blue chips stocks
(that pay dividends, of course) is reasonable, but mid- and
small cap investments should be made through mutual
funds and indices.**

Growth Stocks

Growth stocks are the most popular equities because this
sector represents strong companies with expected rising
sales, profits, and prospects. As a result, the prices of their
stocks may appreciate more rapidly as compared to other sectors. Growth stocks are the ones you usually hear your neigh-
bor bragging about at a cocktail party. Not surprisingly,
growth stocks are also more volatile than other sectors and
often much riskier. <u>Warning:</u> *Rumors abound among growth
stock watchers. Listening too closely may be hazardous to*

your financial health. In fact, listening to closely to <u>rumors</u> about any investments can be hazardous.

Bottom Line: Growth stocks generally do not pay dividends since the company usually reinvests profits back into the company to promote continued growth. Suffice to say, these types of individual equities should *not* make up a huge portion of your portfolio. Conservatively, no more than 6 to 10 percent of your asset allocation should be in large cap growth stocks.

Value Stocks

Value stocks are the ones that no one else wants—at least for now. Value stocks represent companies that are out of favor with current Wall Street trends. These companies may be having problems—anything from inept management to inability to compete in the current market. Not surprisingly, in the overall equity market, value stocks are also cheap compared to growth stocks. Many investors believe that a value stock is a good buy if it is likely that the price will return to what is considered normal after other investors have a chance to rethink their position or the company resolves the problems that may have precipitated the decline in stock value.

That said, however, there is a reason (or reasons) that these stocks are trading at a discount compared to their growth stock cousins. So *before you invest*, make sure you know what those reasons are, and that there is at least a reasonable expectation that any problems will be resolved, preferably in *this* lifetime.

Bottom Line: Your portfolio should include a percentage of value stocks. The addition of value stocks will help decrease volatility and should be balanced against your weighting in growth stocks. A conservative portfolio should include a 6 to 10 percent investment in large cap value stocks.

Domestic versus Foreign

Although foreign companies may mean more lucrative returns, even the savviest investors remain skittish about investing in individual foreign stocks on foreign exchanges. Wise investors (i.e., those who do their homework) can usually recognize a worthwhile overseas investment and take advantage of the opportunity to further diversify their portfolio.

Financial experts have long recognized that international stocks represent added investment opportunity. After all, there are approximately *twenty-one major stock markets outside of the United States* that have *more than a thousand companies of substantial size.* Many of those companies operate in rapidly growing economies and therefore have the potential for high returns on investment.

Investing in foreign markets is also an excellent way to diversify your portfolio. U.S. and foreign shares do not always move in tandem. When one is up, the other may be down, and vice versa. Of course, this does not mean that U.S. and foreign shares always move in opposite directions. Because many countries rely heavily on the United States for imports and exports, they are susceptible to U.S. market shifts. It is a characteristic of the global economy that stocks often move in the same direction, especially when the United States is experiencing a major bear or bull market. Still, historically, U.S. and foreign shares show enough independence so that investing overseas can result in added diversification and possibly improved returns.

Some Additional Comments about Risk

Lest I be accused of understating the risk of international investment, I want to emphasize that the political and economic stability of the country in which you are considering making an investment must be carefully considered before any final decision is made. Buying international stocks when a country is in the middle of political, social, and/or economic upheaval is the very definition of "risky business."

I said earlier that wise investors (i.e., those who do their homework) usually have no trouble recognizing a worthwhile overseas investment opportunity. Let me now add, however—and please do not take this personally—that most investors are just not that wise. In fact, most investors have trouble identifying good investments right here in their own backyard, so to speak. That's why the universe created financial advisors!

Know also that reporting and tax regulations in most foreign countries are, as a rule, far different than regulations in the United States. For example, many foreign companies are *not required* to provide detailed information on company history or current operations to investors. Their accounting procedures may also be very different.

In short, while buying individual international stocks can be an excellent way to balance and diversify your portfolio, doing your homework before making any purchase decisions is critical. Find out as much as you can about the company, its country of origin, and any restrictions or regulations. If after you have carefully examined a particular company as a possible investment, you feel justified in going forward—**stop.** Think hard about whether this investment is indeed worth the risk. Are you in it to make a killing or is further diversification among markets your true goal, as it should be?

With these caveats in mind, however, investors who are patient and willing to do the necessary research may find tremendous rewards in international stocks. Here are a couple of the different types of international investments that are available for your consideration.

American Depository Receipts (ADRs)

Many investors appreciate the possible rewards of buying international stock but are put off by the often convoluted mechanics of buying on a foreign exchange. ADRs can help to simplify this process for you. In addition to offering the potential benefits of portfolio diversification, ADRs are traded on U.S. stock exchanges and can be held in much the same way as ordinary U.S. shares. Also, historically, ADR prices have performed much like the foreign stocks they represent. Still more helpful for the investor is the fact that foreign companies with ADRs issue financial reports that generally conform to U.S. accounting conventions and *most* (though not necessarily all) SEC rules.

Buying foreign stocks on foreign markets is very difficult and individual investors will have a tough time finding a brokerage firm to help them. For most brokerage houses, the process is too expensive and the demand is not high enough to warrant the additional investment in infrastructure.

<u>Bottom Line:</u> If you are going to buy *individual* foreign stocks, use an ADR.

U.S. Multinationals

Before making the decision to buy foreign stocks, investors should look into the possibility of purchasing domestic stocks with exposure to foreign markets. Many U.S. companies generate the majority of revenue from overseas. (Coca-Cola, for instance, generates over 80 percent of its sales outside the U.S.) Thus, buying shares of U.S. multinationals can be an effective way for investors to include a global component in their portfolios.

Foreign investing in U.S. multinationals is a more conservative approach than investing through an ADR, and it lacks the possible correlation to a particular market or country. But U.S. multinationals are an alternative for the more conservative investor.

Bottom Line: Every well-diversified portfolio should include a percentage of international stocks. That said, however, it is important to remember that investing abroad comes with a number of risks including, but by no means limited to, exchange rates, political and economic instability, differences in reporting and tax regulations, etc. This cannot be overstated: Do Your Homework! Make sure you thoroughly understand the risks before deciding on a purchase. Finally, take advantage of the opportunities to access foreign markets using ADRs, international stocks traded on U.S. exchanges, and U.S. multinational corporations. As is almost always the case, the most prudent way to purchase these types of investment vehicles is through professionally managed mutual funds. A conservative growth and income model portfolio should have no more than 3 to 5 percent of its assets in international stocks. This amount can be increased if the trends in certain markets are clear; however, it is generally unwise to allow investment in international stocks to get above 10 to 15 percent of a conservative portfolio.

Utilities

I do not need to tell you what utilities are. You pay for them every month. My purpose here is to give you a perspective on utilities as investment opportunities.

As a rule, utilities provide predictable earnings and cash flow growth both of which are attractive especially to the more cautious risk-averse investor who is looking for safety and income. Utilities that operate in regulated markets (as most do) tend to show more stable earnings and produce higher dividend payments. Again, that makes utilities an attractive option for many—make that most—investors.

Utilities are popular investments because the companies produce services on which we have come to depend. Even when the job market and the overall economy are down and people are cutting back, they usually do not walk around in the dark (if they can help it). They usually do not live without water or heat either (again, if they can help it). Since the demand is always there, the supply is usually there as well.

Thus, the utilities sector is an excellent place to search for companies that pay dividends. In fact, the more you look, the more you are likely to find. Start in your own backyard (literally!) by looking into local water, gas, and electric companies. You send them a check every month. So why should they return the favor now and then?

Bottom Line: Utilities provide predictable stable earnings, cash flow, and depending on the market, comparatively high dividends. If you feel you must buy individual stocks without the benefit of going through a mutual fund or index, this is the area in which to do it.

The REIT Stuff

Equity REITs, which specialize in owning certain types of real estate operations, e.g., apartments, regional malls, office buildings, etc. There are even some super specialized REITs that own nothing but golf courses. (Sunday afternoon retiree/duffers take notice!)

Equity REITs are stocks/trusts that pay dividends that come from the earnings of the trust. As long as the trust returns 90 percent of its earnings to investors in the form of dividends, the trust receives special and prized tax considerations. Trust earnings are not taxed at the corporate level but are only taxed when paid to the shareholder. Thus, REIT dividends are considered interest and, as such, are taxed at ordinary income rates rather than the 15 percent special rate that applies to ordinary dividends. Moreover, since REIT dividends are taxed only once, the payout rates are usually much higher than individual stocks investments.

That is the good news. The less good news is that the equity REIT market can be volatile, with large fluctuations in share price. Even so, considering the usually high dividends, REITs are an excellent choice for investors seeking income.

Experts generally analyze REITs from what is called a top-down perspective, i.e., with a focus on particular market sectors. The value of equity REITs is affected by fluctuations in property supply and demand, job growth, and population. Rising interest rates have a negative effect on REITs since borrowing costs rise and the amount you can earn on a less risky investment (e.g., a CD or T-bill) becomes more competitive. In short, when the demand for riskier income producing investments wanes, the Equity REIT shares may drop in value.

If you are considering investing in equity REITs, look for strong prospects for revenue growth as well as unique strategies for increasing and improving occupancy and, frankly, raising rents.

As with any investment, do your homework. Be sure you know what you are buying. These investments are not without risk. High dividends can be enticing, but wherever there is a chance for major gains, there is an equal if not greater chance for major losses.

Bottom Line: Equity REITs can be excellent opportunities for investment growth and high dividends. Interested investors should proceed with caution, however, since all REITs have unique characteristics that should be fully understood before investing.

Exchange-Traded Funds (ETFs)

ETFs are securities made up of "baskets" of stocks that belong to certain sectors of the market. ETFs are geared to reflect the ups and downs of those baskets of stocks. For example, instead of buying different individual gold stocks, you might choose to invest in a gold ETF that mimics the price movement of a basket of individual gold stocks. Or perhaps, you would prefer a basket of biotechnology stocks or energy or financials. There are as many choices as there are sectors.

Because the "basket" rarely changes, some experts like to refer to ETFs as mini-indices. That characterization may be right or wrong, but from an investor's point of view, it summarizes what ETFs were created to do.

Institutions have been using ETFs for quite a while, but now more and more individual investors are participating. Many different companies have developed these mini-indices, which have names such as Holders, iShares, Vipers, Diamonds, Streettracks, and SPYDRS with more being created every day.

Comparisons between mutual funds and ETFs are inevitable. Here are some of the differences in terms of advantages and disadvantages.

The most obvious difference is that most ETFs are unmanaged and, therefore, will cost you less than a mutual fund in yearly fees. Mutual funds are managed. Investors pay fees for management and fund operation.

ETFs trade like stocks, which means investors can buy and sell them throughout the day. Mutual funds offer daily liquidity; but the price is set once a day after the market closes, and everyone gets the same share price.

ETFs are purchased on the exchanges, like stocks, and there is a commission. Mutual funds have different pricing categories and may have upfront, back end, or no-load fee structures.

ETFs are a particularly effective means of diversifying your portfolio. There are literally hundreds of ETFs covering every major index, all sectors of the equities market (i.e., large, middle, and small caps, growth, value, etc.), and other asset classes, including fixed-income and long-, mid-, and short-term bonds. There are international ETFs as well as specialized ETFs in specific markets (e.g., gold, silver, oil etc.). While it is possible to achieve this level of diversification through mutual funds, the fees might be prohibitively high. In addition, it would be more difficult to assemble "pure sector" portfolios through mutual funds.

In the end, many investors find the ETF to be a cleaner, neater, easier way to add and subtract sectors from their portfolios. As with mutual funds, there are ETFs that encompass every investment category and sector.

Recently, a new breed of ETF has emerged that features active management in an attempt to combine the active management common to mutual funds with the liquidity and sector specific investment possibilities of an ETF. The jury is still out on the performance of this new breed of ETFs.

Nuveen Investments sponsors an excellent Web site, www.ETFconnect.com, for sorting through the wide variety of ETFs available.

Bottom Line: In general, if you are willing to give up active portfolio management, an ETF might be right for you. Earlier, we stated that asset allocation is the primary catalyst in 90 percent portfolio performance. With this in mind, ETFs are a convenient way for investors to structure and adjust their asset allocation needs. ETFs provide a reasonably simple means by which individual investors can add and subtract sectors of the market to and from their portfolios. ETFs are also comparatively easy to understand. Since it is impossible to know in advance whether a mutual fund or individual stock will outperform its index, buying a "basket" may be the best way to go. ETFs can be good substitutes for mutual funds and individual stocks and make excellent additions to your portfolios.

Master Limited Partnerships (MLPs)

MLPs are limited partnerships traded on the exchanges like stocks. Because of their partnership structures, MLPs generally do not pay taxes on the income they earn. Instead the income is passed on to the shareholder. Not only does this mean that the dividends are generally higher than individual stock dividends, it also reduces the cost of capital to the partnership, which increases their competitive advantage.

These partnerships are usually involved in high cash flow, mature operations such as energy, timber, other natural resources, and real estate.

Because a portion of the dividends can be tax-deferred, MLPs may be better suited for individual taxable accounts rather than tax-deferred accounts like IRAs.

Although the tax structure along with the competitive advantage makes MLPs a good choice for many income-oriented investors, there are some risks. (You saw that coming, right?)

As with all investments, you have to do your homework before purchasing an MLP just as you would before purchasing an individual stock. Here are just a few questions for which you should obtain solid answers before investing in an MLP.

- What are the prospects for growth?
- What is the management philosophy on growing the dividend?
- Is there room for dividend growth?
- Has there been a large price swing in the particular sector in which the MLP you are considering is involved?
- Is this a good time to invest in that sector or sectors?
- What other factors, such as the political environment, might precipitate an economic downturn?

Weigh these considerations against the possible advantages of other investment choices before making any final decisions.

Bottom Line: MLPs are a great source of income for retirees. Although not as well understood as REITs or other high income-producing securities, MLPs should be considered if you are comfortable with the structure. They can be a good addition to a well-diversified portfolio.

Closed-End Equity and Income Funds

The structure of closed-end funds is just like an ETF, i.e., a basket of stocks or bonds put together and packaged into one investment. Investors looking for diversification and exposure to a popular market segment may purchase these securities. In addition, these funds are generally unmanaged and trade on the stock exchanges, which make them easy to buy and sell.

Closed-end funds come in hundreds of varieties and may be sector specific. Thus, there could be an Internet closed-end fund or a fund with a specific theme such as the Baby Boomer Aging of America Fund or Corporate Bond Income funds and Tax-free Municipal Income funds. Unlike ETFs, which try to mimic a particular sector, closed-end funds often revolve around themes.

Many closed-end funds borrow money, which they then use to leverage their purchasing power. For example, a fund may borrow short-term at 2 percent and then invest long-term at 5 percent, and the difference—the spread (if you will)—is passed on to the shareholders as additional income. Trying to capitalize on this spread can both help and hurt fund performance. Rising short-term rates may cause the dividends to be cut.

Although attractive to shareholders, this type of leveraging is not without risk as it increases volatility particularly during a time of rising interest rates. Enticed by the potentially high dividends, many investors fail to take this risk factor into account. A blue chip dividend stock fund with leverage is a riskier investment than one that does not employ this leveraging strategy. Similarly, a tax-free leveraged bond fund is a much riskier investment than the individual bond itself.

<u>Bottom Line:</u> Closed-end funds are an investment product that has been used by financial advisors and individual investors alike for years. These funds offer diversification and come in many varieties. Be wary of the use of leveraging, however, as this increases your volatility and risk.

Unit Trusts

Unit trusts are investment products that are packaged around a specific theme or goal. Like closed-end funds and mutual funds, the themes vary widely from growth to income.

Trusts were created to give investors the ability to invest in a basket of stocks or bonds based on the theme of choice. For example, the sponsoring company may decide that an Internet-based trust may be appealing to investors. The sponsor will research and pick a basket of stocks whose businesses are in the Internet sector. The stocks are placed in the trust and held—unmanaged—for a specified period of time, usually one to five years. Because the sponsor does not manage the trust like a mutual fund manager does, the investments are stagnant and remain fixed.

At the end of the time frame, there may be another series available to roll (invest) into or the fund will cash out and the current cash value will be dispersed to the unit holders.

Bottom Line: **Unit trusts are another tool in your arsenal to diversify your portfolio. Whether you are looking for growth or income, there will be a trust available. These investments are unmanaged so whether a stock or bond in the portfolio is doing very well or poorly, it will be held through the life of the fund.**

Pink Sheet and Penny Stocks

How many times have you been offered a "can't miss opportunity" to "get in on the ground floor" by buying stock that is going "through the roof" in twenty-four hours—maybe even sooner?

Everybody is looking for a way to get rich quick. Why else do lottery ticket sales skyrocket—especially when the jackpot hits the $300,000,000 stratosphere? In our heads, we know it won't happen. But we don't buy lottery tickets with our heads. We buy them (yes, I do too once in a while) with our hearts and a childlike (childish?) enthusiasm that comes from "wishing upon a star" and seeing one too many Disney movies when we were growing up.

Well, here's a real and final stock tip. Penny stocks and pink sheet stocks are the "lottery tickets" of the equity investment world. The difference is that with lottery tickets (unless you have completely lost your mind!) you only risk (and lose) a few dollars. With penny and pink sheet stocks the investments are usually much higher and you could lose everything.

Facts:

1. Liquidity in these stocks is poor.
2. They are not traded on any exchange.
3. The information on the companies in which you would be investing is usually impossible to verify.

Bottom Line: Your chances of "getting in on the ground floor" of some fantastic stock deal are perhaps marginally higher than your chances of winning the lottery. When it comes to investing, stick with high quality, dependable, verifiable financial venues. If you want to gamble, go to Vegas. You'll lose less money (I hope!!) and have a lot more fun doing it.

Conclusion

Certainly, there are no rules that forbid you, as an investor, from selecting individual stocks on your own. But if you are even slightly uncomfortable doing this, by all means get help from a professional financial advisor.

For long-term growth and income, your retirement portfolio should definitely include some equity investments that pay dividends. Remember: Principal fluctuation is on paper. **Dividends are cash.** Remember also that equities are one of the best hedges against inflation, and they protect your purchasing power as well. The percentage of equities in your portfolio is a decision you should make working together with your financial advisor to determine how much risk you may need to take and how much you can comfortably stand. When you begin withdrawing from your retirement savings, financial calculators help to determine how many years your next egg may last and how large of an estate you may leave to your heirs. The software provided with this book does just that. Ideally, you want it to last longer than you do. Sound equity investments can help make that possible.

Chapter 5

MUTUAL FUNDS

Mutual funds are one of the most popular and easily managed investments an individual investor can make.

A mutual fund is made up of individual investors who pool their money and choose a professional money manager to make decisions as to what to buy and sell and when. A typical fund may have hundreds of individual investments. At the end of each day, the investment securities are totaled up and divided by the number of shares. A share price, known as a net asset value (NAV), is then is calculated. All transactions by individual investors are done at the end of the day, and each investor gets the same share price whether buying or selling.

Mutual fund companies facilitate the investment (i.e., the buying and selling) process by hiring managers to run various styles of portfolios. If the manager is doing a good job, the NAV of the shares rises. Conversely, the value drops if the manager is not performing well. The share price is calculated daily; and the returns are published in newspapers, financial publications, and on fund company Web sites.

As an investor, you will receive statements from the mutual fund company on the value of your shares as well as periodic performance numbers. All this information makes it easy to track the overall performance of the fund and your investment. Unless you have your head in the sand (which most investors do not), you should be able to spot those investments that are not performing well.

My uncle Bernie has spread his investments out among one hundred funds, giving a little to each to manage. Now, at the end of every month, his new best friend, the U.S. Postman, pulls up with batches of information and data. At first, of course, Uncle Bernie went through it all, but as time went on it became too much to manage. However, the mail kept coming and coming. Now he is trapped in his house, and we have to feed him through the mail slot in his door.

Not really. He does receive so much mail that he is suffering from investor information overload, which has left him unsure about what he really has and what to do with it. The point: Too much of a good thing can spoil the fun. Investing in a limited variety of funds is probably enough for most investors and is much easier to manage.

There are a number of advantages to investing in a mutual a fund or funds. Here are just a few.

- Mutual funds are well regulated, thus providing the investor with excellent protection against any possible fraud.
- Mutual funds facilitate the diversification of assets that is so critical to portfolio performance. Most investors either lack the skill or just do not have the time or resources to continually research and monitor their portfolio. Because a mutual fund invests in hundreds of individual securities, even the failure of one, when spread across the portfolio of the whole,

will have little effect on share price and overall returns.

- Investing in a mutual fund is convenient, easy, and comparatively inexpensive.
- Mutual funds have exceptional liquidity. In short, you can get your money out just as easily as you put it in.

Are there downsides to investing in mutual funds? Of course. Should the <u>entire</u> market in which a particular fund is invested experience a decline in value, the value of mutual fund shares will go down as well. Therefore, even in a mutual fund, investors run the risk of losing their money.

Fact: There are no risk-free investments. Because of the professional money management and diversification, however, mutual fund investors face fewer risks than when buying and selling stocks, bonds, etc., on their own.

Other potential downsides to mutual fund investments include the following:

- Some mutual funds have minimum investment requirements.
- Mutual funds charge administrative fees to cover their expenses. Some also compensate brokers, financial consultants, and/or planners by charging sales commissions or "loads."
- As a rule, the most actively managed mutual fund may sell over 50 percent of the securities in their portfolio in a typical year. If your fund makes a profit on those sales, you, as an investor, will be subject to capital gains tax on the distribution you receive. By law, it must be declared in the year the fund "books" the trade.
- As an investor in a mutual fund, you are depending on the fund managers to make the right choices for

the portfolio. As in all other professions, some fund managers are better than others are. Here is where doing your homework before investing pays off. Make sure the fund you select has hired, historically, the best highest-producing fund managers.

If you are about to retire or have recently done so, I recommend mutual funds for the equity portion of your investments and the riskier bond portfolios. (More about this later in chapter 7.)

Types of Mutual Funds

There are as many different types of mutual funds as there are investors with different investment objectives. It may be helpful to engage the services of an advisor to learn as much as possible about the different funds before making any investment decisions. Your local library is also an excellent source for information that will help you make an informed decision.

Each type of mutual fund has different risks and rewards. As a rule of thumb, the higher the potential return, the higher the risk of loss.

Fact (**worth repeating**): There are no risk-free investments.

The objective of each mutual fund is usually clearly stated. The title of the fund itself is generally a reliable arbiter of the goal of the fund. For example, the goal of the (hypothetical) ABC Growth Fund is growing assets, while the goal of the (also hypothetical) ABC Income Fund is providing income.

Note: As far as I know, there are no actual mutual fund companies with these names. I made them up just to use as examples. So please do not go looking for them to invest!

Although there are many categories of mutual funds, the most popular are equity funds (stocks), fixed-income funds (bonds), and money market funds (cash).

Equity Funds

The largest category of mutual funds is the equity funds. As a rule, the primary objective of an equity fund is long-term capital growth. Investors should be aware, however, that there are many different types of equity funds simply because there are many different types of equities.

As stated earlier, because of the professional management and excellent diversification, which can limit volatility, many savvy investors use mutual funds for the equity portion of their investments. This is by no means a put-down of individual purchases of individual stocks, e.g., blue chips. Rather, it is to stress the advisability of mutual funds because of the advantage that comes with professional money management. Your goal, after all, is as smooth a ride as possible during your retirement years and that means maintaining the asset allocations that suit your needs and supports your lifestyle. Are you a roller-coaster kind of a person? Is the thought of a beach boy (or girl) pouring cool water on your sun-drenched feet as you lie under an umbrella sipping a fruit-laden drink (with or without booze) more to your taste? (The beach thing works for me.) In short, how much risk you are willing to take is one (though not the only) way of deciding which equity funds are best for you.

Equity funds are easily bought and sold; and rebalancing is simple should, for example, one fund become too large a part of your portfolio, an eventuality that is more likely to occur with equities as they grow than with bonds.

Initially, equity funds are classified or defined based on the size of the companies in which they hold stock. Large capitalization (or large-cap) refers to large companies, whereas middle-sized capitalization (or mid-cap) refers to middle-sized companies, and small capitalization (or small-cap) to smaller companies. The investment style of the manager is categorized in terms of value versus growth or a blend of each. Sub-sectors of investment may include biotechnology, energy, and international sectors. Thus, for example, you may find a small-cap international value fund and a large-cap energy fund.

Now let us turn to the broader categories of equity funds and the potential risks and rewards of each.

Growth Funds

As the name implies, the goal of this type of fund is growing your capital. Investing primarily in common stocks with the potential for appreciation, the primary objective of these funds is to increase the value of your assets rather than to generate an income flow. Such growth will help to offset the negative effects of inflation. Any diversified portfolio should have a good growth fund as part of its asset allocation. You will hear most about these funds. They are sexy, and they sell. Although they are marketed to attract high rollers, low rollers (i.e., more risk-averse investors like you and me) would be wise to have some money committed to a growth equity fund. Since growth funds are designed to grow capital rather than provide dividends. We will include this type of fund in your portfolio's allocation as an inflation hedge. (10 to 25 percent of a portfolio)

There are several subgroups among growth equity funds.

Aggressive Growth Funds

Aggressive growth funds invest primarily in the stock of smaller companies with the potential for higher appreciation. Recommendation: No more than 5 percent of a portfolio should be invested in these funds (unless, of course, you are the "Evil Knieval" of your investment crowd!)

Emerging Market Equity Funds

These funds are very aggressive and invest in equities of companies based in the less well-developed regions of the world. Again, no more than 5 percent of a portfolio should be invested in these funds.

Global Equity Funds

These funds invest in companies all over the world including the United States. Some can be more aggressive than others can. A more conservatively invested fund would be a good choice for the equity allocation. (5 to 10 percent of a portfolio)

Growth and Income Funds

These funds invest in equities that pay dividends (typically 1 to 2 percent, which is a small but steady income stream), have the potential for long-term growth, and provide a hedge against inflation.

A mighty trio, indeed, and thus an excellent choice for retirees. (25 to 40 percent of a portfolio)

International Equity Funds

International equity funds invest primarily outside the United States. Since the United States is only part of the overall market, exposure to world markets is a necessity for any well-diversified portfolio. (5 to 10 percent of a portfolio)

Regional Equity Funds

These funds invest in companies in specific regions around the world (e.g., Europe and Latin America) or in specific countries within the various regions of the world. If you have a strong opinion about the potential for economic growth, and thus a better investment return, in a particular region, then a small allocation to a regional fund in your portfolio may be in order. That said, however, more diversified global funds are a better choice for most investors. (No more than 5 percent of a portfolio should be invested in a regional equity fund.)

Sector Equity Funds

These funds invest in specific sectors of the market such as technology, finance, or real estate. Because different sectors tend to come in and out of favor more often than the general market, sector funds tend to be more volatile than more diversified funds.

As a rule, a sector "bet" is a poor idea for those entering retirement. If you have a strong feeling one way or the other about a particular sector, a very small portion of your portfolio could be allocated to that sector. Use caution, however. For most people, especially retirees, I would not recommend investing in a sector equity fund.

Bond/Income Funds

Income funds are designed to do precisely what their name implies: generate a regular stream of income. For mutual funds, the terms *fixed-income*, *bond*, and *income* are interchangeable. Fund holdings may appreciate and depreciate, but the primary objective of the bond/income fund is to provide a steady cash flow to investors. Not surprisingly, conservative investors and retirees are particularly attracted to these types of funds.

The risks associated with a particular bond fund vary depending on how and where they invest. A fund specializing in high-yield junk bonds is naturally a much riskier investment than a fund that invests primarily in government securities. Investors should also remember that the value of nearly all bond funds fluctuates with interest rates. If interest rates go up, the value of the fund goes down. Should you choose then to liquidate any or all of your investment, you may not receive your principal back. This is one major difference between investing in bond *funds* versus *individual* bonds. A bond has a future, i.e., the issuer has promised to return your principal to you at some point. <u>A bond *fund* makes no such promise</u>.

Know also that when interest rates are rising, the principle in a bond fund usually falls. Conversely, when interest rates are falling, the value of a fund may rise. Therefore, the current economic cycle and the current and future direction of interest rates should have a bearing on the types of bond funds in which you choose to invest. As a rule of thumb: The longer the average maturity of a portfolio, the more volatile it will be. Duration is a better measure of a portfolios reaction to rates. The lower the stated duration, the less volatile it should be. The average maturity and duration are easy to find and are usually listed in any detailed information sheet about the fund.

With these things in mind, the following recommendations are based on risk/reward as it pertains to the benefits mutual funds may provide versus the individual bond in the same category. These recommendations remind me a little of blind dates—may look good on the surface, but on closer inspection, may not be your cup of tea, after all. Different strokes for different folks, as the saying went. Just be sure you know how the returns are being generated before you invest. Here I have provided a simple analysis just as a starting point. Do your homework before you invest.

Money Market Funds

A money market fund is probably one of the safest places for your money if you are an investor. The money market consists of short-term debt instruments—mostly T- bills, corporate notes, etc. The returns are not very high, but the risk of losing your principle is very low. A typical return is approximately twice the amount you would earn in a regular checking/savings account. A money market fund is a great place to park short-term capital that you wish to keep liquid. Most retirees will have some money in a money market fund. It is precautionary—sort of a belt-and-suspenders type of investment.

Corporate Bond Funds

Corporate bond funds come in ultra short-term, short-term, intermediate-term, long-term, and blended maturities. These funds seek a high level of income by investing in corporate bonds of individual companies. There is a direct correlation between the length of maturity of the bonds and the amount of interest these funds pay. A long-term corporate bond fund will pay a higher rate of interest than a short-term corporate bond fund.

Before investing in a corporate bond fund, make sure you understand the current economic interest rate cycle. ("Paging, the fed chairman. Paging, the fed chairman. Please call your office.") Compare the yield on the funds you are considering to yields on *individual investments* that have a stated maturity date. Make sure that you are being adequately compensated for the ***absence of the promise*** to pay back your principal at a later date if you choose to invest in a corporate bond fund. ***If the timing and yields are right***, corporate bond funds are great income-producing investments and should be part of your portfolio.

Global Bond Funds

These funds invest in bonds from all over the world and have exposure to a wide variety of economies and interest rate cycles. In addition to the ordinary risks associated with domestic bond funds, global bond funds carry regional political risks as well as risks associated with currency fluctuations. What happens if the local currency is devalued in relation to the U.S. dollar? What happens if the government collapses? Although the majority of bond fund managers are aware of these risks and take appropriate action to limit them, investors should remember that some bond managers make better decisions than others do.

As a rule, global bonds should only be purchased through a mutual fund, which limits the risk through professional management while bringing diversification to the portfolio. In short, although global bond funds can be part of your asset allocations, most investors should avoid buying individual global bonds.

U.S. Government Bond Funds

Available in short-term, intermediate-term, long-term as well as blended average maturities, government bond funds provide income by investing in a diversified portfolio of government bonds. Since the funds are backed by the full faith and credit of the U.S. government, the risks for investors are slight.

Even so, this is a case where investors might be better off buying individual bonds, taking into the account the fact that mutual funds carry fees and that those fees are deducted from the yield, which may be lower when compared to other income producing investments. Thus, investors would be wise to do some comparison shopping in the bond market to see if another investment will provide the same yield but with the promise that the principle will be returned at a specific date of maturity. Remember: Bond mutual funds come with no such promise.

High-Yield Funds

High-yield funds are highly risky since they invest in companies whose bonds are below investment grade. Because the risk is so high, the yields are also higher than other bond funds. In a well-diversified portfolio, a good high-yield bond fund, although more risky, can add yield and additional diversification. Note: Investors should never buy high-yield bonds on their own. As individual investments, they are far too risky. If, however, you discover that a high-yield fund is paying substantially more than you can get in other investments, then you may want to allocate a portion of your bond assets to the high-yield market. If the fund is not paying substantially more, then the investment is not worth the risk. So play your cards close to the vest, but *do* play them when appropriate.

Mortgage-Backed Funds

Mortgage-backed funds invest in mortgage-backed securities. As a rule, the underlying investments are rated AAA. Because these funds are highly affected by the direction of interest rates, investors must pay close attention to the interest rate cycle before making a decision to purchase. That said, however, mortgage-backed funds are considered safe and often have a somewhat higher yield, so most retirees should consider them.

Diversified Bond Funds

These funds buy a little bit of everything—diversifying among many different types of fixed- income securities. Often they mix in equity securities as well. These bond funds are a solid choice for a portion of your portfolio as the risks drop with the additional diversification.

Hedge Funds

Once upon a time, the availability of these types of funds was limited to the wealthy. Today they are more widely available. Hedge funds largely remain unregulated management vehicles. As is the case with mutual funds, hedge funds hire professional managers to make decisions on what to buy and sell. Be aware, however, that in hedge funds, investments can be made in any type of security and very often, you, as the investor, are unaware of the decisions made by the fund manager. This lack of oversight makes the risks associated with hedge fund investments greater than with other types of investments. Think of hedge funds as the wild west of investment choices.

Hedge funds have garnered a lot of press because they have recently produced better returns than other more traditional investments. If your objective is to increase returns through riskier investments such as a hedge fund, then I would suggest an alternative: the fund-of-funds approach.

Fund of Funds

In this type of investment vehicle, a mutual fund or a brokerage company pulls together a group of hedge funds with each manager specializing in a particular area of the market and packages them as one large diversified fund investment. This makes the fund-of-funds approach a perfect choice for scaredy-cat investors (like me) who want to invest in a hedge fund. The additional diversification helps to eliminate some of the volatility and the oversight risks as investors get the benefit of professional management as well. Investors who are looking for a more conservative way to participate in the unregulated hedge fund market will be attracted to this investment option. In fact, most investors could probably benefit from the fund of fund approach.

If you are among the more sophisticated of investors who are looking for extra special returns and who are able to do the research and willing to take the extra risk—risk that is sometimes hard to recognize until it is realized, then hedge funds may deliver.

Know also that the fund-of-funds approach has been put together for other investment options including mutual funds, closed-end funds, and unit trusts.

Municipal Bond Funds

Available in short-term, intermediate-term, long-term, and blended average maturities, municipal bond funds generate income by investing in a portfolio of municipal bonds that are free from federal income tax. These funds may also invest state-specific bond funds, e.g., the New York State municipal bond fund. State-specific bond funds may be free of state and local taxes as well. So find out if your state has such a bond fund. Most large states do.

Although these funds pay less interest than other taxable bond funds, once you calculate the after-tax yield, the money left in your pocket after you pay income tax could make these funds a competitive investment choice.

Municipal bond funds are particularly attractive to those in higher tax brackets. The mutual fund company (or your financial advisor) can calculate the after-tax yield for you. (See chapter 3.) Compare the yield on these funds to the yield from individual municipal bonds. If you are being adequately compensated for the risk associated with the ***absence of a promise*** to return your principle at a specific date, then the bond mutual fund may be the best choice. If you are ***not*** being adequately compensated for that risk, individual bonds are the better option.

High-Yield Municipal Bond Funds

High-yield municipal bond funds have the same advantages of regular municipal bond funds; however, the high-yield funds invest in a portfolio of poorly rated riskier bonds. The potential yield is higher, but so is the risk. While default risk with municipal bonds is low, it does happen. With that in mind, there is a place in a well-diversified portfolio for a high-yield municipal bond fund investment.

Balanced Funds

Chocolate or vanilla? Chocolate or vanilla? Are you having trouble making up your mind? Then a balanced fund may be for you. Balanced funds strive to achieve a balanced mix of capital appreciation and income. To achieve this objective, balanced funds invest in some combination of fixed-income and equities, usually with a percentage weighted toward one or the other, e.g., 60 percent equities and 40 percent fixed-income.

Although this type of fund is fine for most portfolios, funds consisting of either *all bonds* or *all equities* may be preferable. It is my personal view that a manager focusing on one sector is likely to perform better than a manager trying to handle two sectors. Additionally, not all balanced funds are the same. Some take on much more risk that others and that risk is not as easily categorized, as is the risk associated with single sector funds. That said, however, many investors are very happy with their balanced funds and you might be too.

Asset-Allocation Funds

This is a type of fund in which the portfolio is aiming to broadly diversify itself. One stop asset allocation for the investor. With the asset allocation fund, the portfolio manager is free to change the investment ratio depending on economic conditions and/or a particular business cycle. It is the "pinch of this and dash of that" approach to creating what the manager thinks is the ultimate allocation pie. Easy, diversified and professionally managed.

Global/International Funds

An international (or foreign) fund restricts its investments to those outside your home country. Global funds invest around the world, including your home country. Global/international funds are riskier because of the volatility of foreign countries and currencies and the potential for political instability. That said, however, as part of a well-balanced portfolio, these funds could reduce risk by virtue of the increase in diversification. In addition, you get to say that you invest globally, and that is bound to impress somebody.

Sector Funds / Specialty Funds

This type of fund is usually too broad to fit into a specific classification. It may, for example, feature investments that are concentrated in a particular sector of the economy such as financial, technology, health, etc. (Remember the scene in *The Graduate* when someone whispered to the young Dustin Hoffman "Just remember one word: *plastics*.") Sector funds can be extremely volatile. In short, you can win big, but you may also lose big.

Regional Funds

These funds focus on a specific area of the world, e.g., Brazil versus the whole of Latin America. Regional funds make it easier for investors who want to buy stock in foreign countries—something that may be difficult and expensive to do under normal conditions. As with the sector funds, the risks are as high, if not higher, than the potential gain.

Socially Responsible Funds

These funds invest only in companies that meet the criteria of certain guidelines or beliefs. Socially responsible funds rarely invest in industries such as tobacco, alcoholic beverages, weapons, or nuclear power. The objective of this type of fund is to obtain competitive performance while adhering to certain philosophies. Before buying in, however, be sure to check the numbers to see how well the fund manager has performed with a reduced pool of investment choices. (Warning: Your "socially responsible" side may take a turn for the more self-interested, especially during a bull market.)

Index Funds

Index funds replicate the performance of a broad market index such as the S&P 500. Index fund investors assume that most managers are unlikely to beat the market. Thus, an index fund merely replicates the market return. Investors benefit from low fees, and asset allocation is easily achieved, as there is an index to represent almost any sector. Adjustments can also be made easily by selling part of one index and adding to another. Number crunchers among you will like these funds for their low operational expenses.

Life Cycle Funds

This is a relatively new type of fund. It is designed to appeal to retirees who do not want to lose sleep over the seemingly insurmountable intricacies of portfolio management and selecting the right investments. Thanks to the life cycle fund, investing for your retirement does not have to be complicated.

Known also as "age-based" or "target-date" funds, life cycle funds are run by companies that specialize in handling the details of portfolio balance and structure (equity versus fixed-income). Investors in life cycle funds are assured that asset allocation is automatically adjusted in a more conservative direction as they reach their expected retirement date. In short, if you are the kind of investor who is inclined to say, "Oh, you do it!" then the life cycle fund is for you.

To give you a better understanding of how life cycle funds work and whether such a fund might be a good investment for you, we have compared funds operated by two well-known companies. (To avoid the perception of any type of endorsement of either fund, we refer to the companies as Company A and Company B.)

The life cycle fund operated by Company A is directed toward those who plan to retire within five to ten years of 2030. As of September of last year, the asset mix for this fund was approximately 47 percent equity index fund, approximately 41 percent bond index fund, 8 percent Pacific equity fund, and 4 percent European equity index fund.

Compare this to the asset allocation for the fund, managed by Company B, but for those who plan to retire within five to ten years of 2015, i.e., *fifteen years sooner.* The asset allocation for this fund is approximately 49 percent bond market index, approximately 39 percent equity market fund, approximately 7 percent European equity index fund, approximately 3 percent Pacific equity fund, and approximately 2 percent inflation-protected securities fund.

As you can see, asset allocation in the fund for those who plan to retire in 2015 is more conservative with more fixed-income assets and the inclusion of inflation-protected securities.

Note also that Company B's more conservative fund uses inflation-protected securities to protect the portfolio against the impact of inflation on investment returns. This is an important consideration for the investor, and one that is not included in Company B's fund management approach.

Investors should also be aware that the same retirement date does not automatically translate into the same asset allocation, although the information provided from different funds could be easily misconstrued in this manner. Mutual fund companies may and do have different opinions of what allocation should be used. One company may have 75 percent stocks, another thinks 60 percent is better. This difference is significant. This is where evaluating different life cycle funds can get to be a bit complicated. However, it is worth your time in terms of helping you decide how much risk you are willing to take.

If necessary, engage the services of a financial planner to help you evaluate the level of risk involved before investing in a particular fund.

It should also be noted that life cycle funds only make sense if the majority of your retirement savings are in only one fund. Adding more funds or investments could result in the wrong asset allocation for your retirement savings and a portfolio that is not well balanced. Remember: *Over 90 percent* of the performance of your portfolio investments is predicated on how the assets are allocated.

Be aware also that life cycle funds are not known as strong income producers, although some do show enough income to warrant consideration. In general, however, life cycle funds are targeted toward those who are building up to retirement.

To summarize, life cycle funds have gained popularity because they are simple and comparatively sensible. The right life cycle fund can take the worry out of retirement investing and allow the investor a measure of peace of mind, which in the end may be the most valuable asset a retiree can have.

A-B-C Easy as 1, 2, 3: Load or No Load—Which Is Right for You?

Now that we have covered the major types of funds, let's talk a bit about fees.

Fee-wise, mutual funds are broken down into two categories: those to which the investor must pay a fee for purchase and those to which the investor pays no such fee. Be aware that the presence or absence of a fee is only one criterion for selecting a fund. If, for example, you are considering a fund that charges a fee, but has produced superior returns that seem likely to continue, then paying the fee makes sense.

Load Funds

These funds charge investors a fee to purchase shares. As a rule, load funds are offered through financial advisors and the fee you pay is compensation for the advisor's help. Financial professionals are paid in a number of different ways, of which this is just one. See chapter 8 for a further discussion of this topic.

For load funds, fees are broken down into three share classes usually called A class, B class, or C class.

An A share class charges an *upfront* commission—usually higher than B or C share class. Also, the owner of an A share pays lower ongoing yearly fees than do the owners of B or C shares. So depending on the load, the difference in fee, and on how long you own it, the upfront A share commission may be the least expensive way to purchase a particular fund.

As a rule of thumb, if you expect to own the shares for six years or more, then the A share class is probably the cheapest in the long run.

Although B shares do not charge an upfront fee, they do charge a higher yearly fee and a commission if you sell it within six years (in most cases). Called a declining back-end fee, that commission is typically 5 percent for the first year, 4 percent in the second, then three, two, and one until it eventually reaches zero. After a period of time, usually seven years, the shares revert to the A class at which point you begin to receive the benefits of the lower yearly expenses associated with the A share class.

Note: B shares are being phased out because the SEC concluded that other types of breaks in fees were being ignored.

C shares also do not charge an upfront fee to purchase. In addition, C shares only charge between 1 and 2 percent in back-end fees during the first year if you sell.

That said, however, C shares have the highest yearly fees. Therefore, if you plan to hold them a long time, know that it will be by far the most expensive way to purchase a fund even if at the beginning it seems like the least.

Right of Accumulation

Every load fund offers a break on fees the more money you invest. These *breakpoints* are different for every fund company but typically begin at about $25,000, then $50,000, then $100,000, and so on. Here is how it works.

As you invest in the A share and you add money, the upfront load (fee) declines, the more money you put in. Suppose, for example, you invest $20,000, pay a 5 percent sales load, and then later invest another $20,000. The load at the second investment would drop to 4.5 percent. By the time you invested $100,000, it may have dropped to 2 percent.

So if you are investing in load mutual funds, it is to your financial advantage to pool your assets under one fund company's stable of funds rather than to spread your investments around. In addition, you benefit from professional assistance at an increasing discount over time, and you can take advantage of the breakpoints when they are available.

Letters of Intention

A letter of intention is a pledge to purchase a certain amount of a fund within a specific time frame (usually thirteen months) to take immediate advantage of the breakpoint, as if you were making a large upfront purchase.

Suppose, for example, you have $20,000 today to purchase a mutual fund, but you know you will have an additional $50,000 to invest later in the year. A letter of intent will allow you to invest the $20,000 now and receive the breakpoint as if you had invested the whole $70,000 upfront, thereby allowing you to take advantage of any breakpoints now instead of later. If you later renege on your promise, you would be charged back what you would have paid on the initial $20,000. It is like saying, give me a break now and I promise to send you more later. If you ask, the answer will be "yes".

Conclusion

Mutual funds are, by and large, a great way for individuals to invest. Investing in a mutual fund is convenient and easy and there are thousands of different types of mutual funds investors may choose. (Please remember my "Uncle Bernie.")

The best mutual funds are well managed by highly skilled financial experts experienced in selecting the right stocks, securities, bonds, etc., for the portfolio. By selecting a diversified portfolio of mutual funds, you might be able to diversify risk though asset allocation. While one security may decrease in value in response to a particular market trend, in a well-balanced portfolio, another fund is likely to respond to the same trend by showing an increase in value. This means that over time the general trend of the whole portfolio is likely to be toward a steady increase in overall value.

Mutual funds are well regulated thus providing the investor with excellent protection against any possible fraud.

Finally, mutual funds have exceptional liquidity.

Yes, there are disadvantages. Mutual funds charge administrative fees to cover expenses. If your fund makes a profit on transactions, you will have to pay capital gains tax on the income you receive. As an investor, you are depending on fund managers to make the right choices. Most of the time they do but occasionally they do not. Dare I repeat this for emphasis: **There are no risk-free investments. (That means you can lose money.)**

However, the bottom line is the advantages of investing in mutual funds far outweigh the disadvantages. For the majority of retirees, mutual funds are a smart choice.

Chapter 6

Annuities

Most retirees or those about to enter retirement have at least one (if not all) of the following concerns:

1. Protecting their savings,
2. Creating and protecting their retirement income stream, and
3. Protecting their heirs.

Together these three concerns come down to one underlying issue: *risk management*. Properly invested, annuities can be a significant anecdote to these problems.

An annuity is a written contract between you and an insurance company. As an investment designed for retirement, the contract allows you to potentially accumulate funds that will be returned to you as lifetime income payments.

Immediate or Variable/Fixed or Variable Which Annuity Is Right for You?

There are two main categories of annuities: immediate and deferred. Within each of these, there are two subcategories: fixed and variable.

Immediate Annuity

Immediate annuities are financial instruments designed to provide an income stream in retirement. Needless to say, their popularity is increasing daily.

In purchasing an immediate annuity, you make a one-time payment to an insurance company. Based on a variety of factors including but not limited to your age, the mortality table, and the period of time over which you wish to guarantee income, the insurance company will calculate the amount you are to receive. As an example, you may deposit $100,000 with the insurance company with the promise they will send you $800 a month for the rest of your life.

Age

Using a mortality table, the insurance company will determine your average life expectancy. For example, a sixty-five-year-old male, on average, may expect to live another seventeen years. This time period is used in the calculation to determine the amount of the investor's income check.

Interest Rates

Current interest rates are another factor the insurance company uses to calculate how much you will receive. Interest rates are used to determine what return the insurance company can expect from your investment. Those earnings are also used to calculate the amount of your income stream.

Disbursement

The length of time you would like the insurance company to provide income is another major factor in determining your income payment. There are many choices available.

If you elect to receive payments over *your* lifetime, it will be one amount. If you elect to receive payments over your lifetime *and* your spouse's, (i.e., joint and survivor), the dollar amount you receive will be different. Still other options guarantee payment over specific time periods, e.g., five, ten, or even twenty years.

Fixed-Rate Immediate Annuity

With a fixed-rate immediate annuity, you know exactly and in advance how much income you are going to receive. The amount is stated in your contract. Income from annuities is tax deferred, i.e., it will be taxed upon withdrawal at ordinary income tax rates.

Choosing to receive payments over your lifetime is, frankly, a calculated bet on how long you will live. You may live longer than the insurance company's mortality table predicts, which will mean a higher total disbursement. If, on the other hand, you die sooner than the mortality table predicted, the total disbursement will of course be less. Note: Should you die soon after the purchase of the annuity, the income stops, and the balance of the principal will ***not*** be dispersed to your heirs. Clearly, the lifetime payment option would not be a good choice for someone who is very old or sick.

Variable Immediate Annuity

With the variable immediate annuity, your income will fluctuate based on the performance of the investment options you choose. The investment options (also called sub-accounts) behave a lot like mutual funds. Variable immediate annuities are designed to increase your income over time by growing your principal. Of course, if they do not succeed, your income may drop. Thus, there is more risk involved with the variable immediate annuity than with the fixed-rate annuity.

An important caveat: With both the fixed and variable immediate annuities, you give up ready and immediate access to the principal. So make sure you do not invest more than you can afford to live without.

Additionally, transfers between annuity sub-accounts are tax-free. If your asset allocation models change, you will be able to adjust the annuity allocations without a capital gains/loss consequence.

Bottom Line: **Immediate annuities are becoming more popular as retirees look to supplement other sources of income such as Social Security and pensions. There is great security in knowing that a check will be coming in every month for many years to come. That said, however, it is vital that you do your homework before buying an immediate annuity. Certainly if you are in poor health, this is not a viable option.**

Variable Annuity

Fixed-Rate Variable Annuity

With a fixed-rate variable annuity, you invest your capital with an insurance company that promises to pay you interest and to return your capital at an agreed-upon future date, much like a bond.

The safety of your investment is determined by the credit rating of the insurance company, once again, much like a bond. Make sure the insurance company you choose is rated AA or higher. Rule of thumb: Invest in the best. After all, you are choosing this investment option, in part, for safety. Do not compromise on this issue.

Fixed-rate variable annuities, like all annuities, offer the advantage of tax deferral. When you withdraw the money, profits will be taxed at ordinary income tax rates. If you choose to reinvest, no current tax is owed. This must be considered when comparing the rates on fixed annuities to other fixed-income investments. So shop around and compare before you buy!

Know also that choices of rates and maturities vary from company to company. Consulting a financial advisor before making a final decision is, as always, prudent since he or she should have access to many insurance providers, making it easy to compare current rates.

Bottom Line: **Fixed-rate annuities provide a predictable source of income during retirement. One big advantage is income tax deferral should you choose not to take the income but instead to reinvest and allow your earnings to compound. Invest when the rates are better than with other investment options. Remember too that rates ebb and flow. Do not *assume* other choices such as CDs and bonds are paying any more or less. Investigate before you buy.**

Variable Annuity

With the types of annuities described thus far, the investor knows ahead of time, at a minimum, what the return and income stream would be. With the variable annuity, however, the return is *variable* and unknown.

Your money is invested in sub-accounts, which, like mutual funds, are professionally managed and invest in stocks, bonds, and a variety of other market sectors. You may choose the sub-account(s) you prefer just as you may choose among mutual funds. If they do well, you will have more money in the pot. If they do not, you will have less.

Although the variable annuity can offer a guaranteed income payment based on your initial investment, the primary goal is to grow capital to a higher level, which, at some point, you can turn into a *larger* income stream.

The primary difference between a variable annuity and a mutual fund, aside from the tax deferral advantage of the annuity, is that you can also purchase guarantees, called **riders**, to protect yourself against potential declines in your annuity value. There are many different types of riders. Consider each one carefully before making a purchase as each comes with an additional cost along with the benefits.

Bottom Line: Variable annuities are an excellent choice if you are primarily interested in growing your portfolio for your heirs while at the same time providing income should you need it. They are best suited for investors who can withstand some volatility. Speak with a financial specialist before you invest.

Variable Annuity Riders

There are two different classes of riders: death benefits and living benefits. As the names imply, death benefits take effect upon your death, while living benefits can apply while you are still living. Know also that, while some riders are included in an annuity contract, others must be purchased separately. No two contracts are the same so do not assume a rider is included. It must be stated in the contract.

Death Benefits

Standard Death Benefit Rider

This is the most common rider and is included in almost all annuity contracts as part of the purchase. It guarantees that your beneficiaries will receive the cash value or premium, whichever is greater, upon your death.

Suppose, for example, that you invest $100,000 in a variable annuity contract, and that you die when the value has grown to $200,000. Under a standard death benefit, your beneficiaries will receive $200,000, i.e., the current value of the annuity. Suppose the initial investment of $100,000 has dropped to $50,000 by the time of your death. In that event, your beneficiaries would receive the original amount of your investment, i.e., $100,000.

The only downside here is that you have to die to take advantage of the rider. Not a happy prospect, to be sure, but such planning is vital for the protection of your beneficiaries. See example A.

Example A

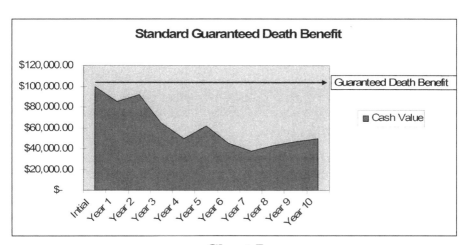

Chart 7
Source: AXA Equitable Life Accumulator
Variable Annuity

Annual Ratchet (or Step Up) Death Benefit Rider

The annual ratchet (or step up) death benefit rider guarantees that your beneficiaries will receive the account value at the time of your death **or** the highest account value on any contract purchase anniversary, whichever is higher. Let us look at an example.

Suppose that on January 1 you invested $100,000 in a variable annuity contract. One year later, it has grown in value to $200,000, but then begins to slowly decline in value to a point where, two years later, it is down to $50,000. In the event of your death, at that point, we already know that under the guaranteed death benefit rider your beneficiaries would receive either the current value or the initial investment amount, whichever is higher.

Under the annual ratchet death benefit rider, however, the insurance company will look back through the anniversary dates of purchase, and if, at an anniversary, in this case January 1, the value of the annuity was higher than your initial investment and current cash value, then your beneficiaries will receive that amount instead. In this case, the highest value ever reached was $200,000. That would be what your beneficiaries would receive. See example B.

Suffice to say that given these riders, the very powerful advantages of the variable annuity over an ordinary mutual fund for which no such riders are available, are clear.

Put another way, imagine your spouse calling your broker or mutual fund company after your death requesting that a check be sent for the highest amount your account ever reached, which just happened to have occurred in the year 2000, before the market crashed. Care to guess what your broker (or mutual fund) would say? Yet with an annuity, you can have this option.

There is more.

Example B

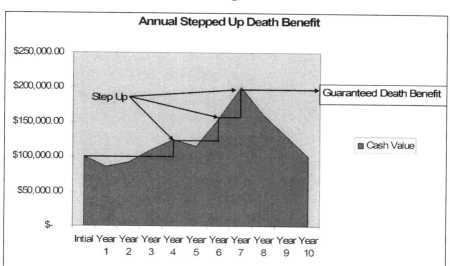

Chart 8
Source: AXA Equitable Life Accumulator Variable
Annuity

Annual Step-Up Plus a Percentage Roll-Up Rider

Suppose, unlike the previous example, your account history when reviewed showed that there had been no rise in value over the years and no gain in value at anniversary? In other words, the market was flat. Under the annual step-up plus percentage roll-up rider, your beneficiaries are promised a guaranteed minimum rate of return on investment, which varies from company to company, but is usually between 4 and 6 percent annually. Example C.

It is like having two horses in the race for retirement. The 6 percent or the market, whichever works out best. Two horses are better than one.

Example C

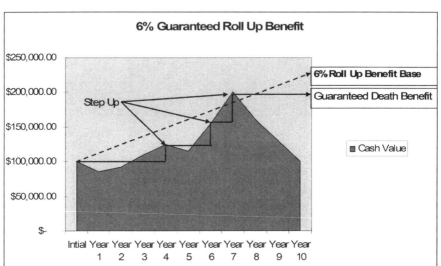

Chart 9
Source: AXA Equitable Life Accumulator
Variable Annuity

Put simply, a variable annuity with the guaranteed death benefit rider plus the annual step-up death benefit rider plus the annual percentage roll-up rider is one of the best guarantees of financial security your beneficiaries can have. Assuming you stay fully invested and make no early withdrawals, the only way your beneficiaries can lose is if the insurance company goes out of business. If you did your homework and picked the strongest possible company from which to purchase, that is not likely to happen.

Now enough about what happens if you die. Let us talk about what happens while you are alive and kicking.

Living Benefits

Protecting your beneficiaries is fine, and most people certainly want to do it. Suppose something happens and you need money now—for a medical emergency, to protect your lifestyle, to protect your kids during a divorce settlement? What are your choices? There are several.

Annuitization

Annuitization is gaining in popularity as more and more retirees want a guaranteed lifetime income stream. Here is how it works. You forfeit your investment, at its current value, to the insurance company, which in turn guarantees you an income stream for the rest of your life. There will be no lump sum payment of any amount upon your death. Should you die prematurely, in most cases, this guarantee includes an income stream that would go to your beneficiaries for a minimum of ten to twenty years.

In short, annuitization means you know, in advance, what your income stream will be. That said, however, many financial experts advise against annuitization because the rate of return is very low. Currently only about 2 percent of investors choose annuitization. However, that percentage is expected to rise as the guaranteed income for life option begins to look more and more attractive particularly to those who went through the stock market bursts at the beginning of this decade.

Systematic Withdrawal

Systematically withdrawing money from your annuity account over time is a common way to begin creating a retirement income stream. You may withdraw a certain dollar amount every month, quarter, or year; or you may choose to withdraw a percentage of your assets. In some annuity contracts, withdrawals may affect other guarantees so make sure you understand how your contract works before you decide on a particular strategy.

Guaranteed Income Benefit

This works the same as the annual ratchet death benefit with annual percentage roll-up rider. Suppose, for example, you invest $100,000 in a variable annuity. Over time the value of the account increases to $200,000 but slowly declines to $50,000 perhaps. Under the guaranteed income benefit rider, you can begin to receive income based on the highest level the account value ever reached on anniversary.

Suppose that investment return amounts to an increase of only 3 percent per year? Since the annual percentage roll-op allows you to collect at a rate of 4 to 6 percent per year, you would be entitled to the higher income amount. Just pick up the phone, call the insurance company, and tell them to turn on your income. It's (almost) that simple. Example D.

Example D

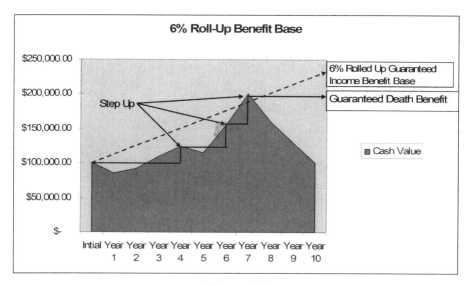

Chart 10
Source: AXA Equitable Life Accumulator
Variable Annuity

Maximizing Income Generation

The withdrawal benefits from annuities vary from company to company but most insurance companies have variations on the same themes. One may annuitize at a higher income level than another. One may offer a 6 percent Living Benefit Guarantee and one only 5 Percent.

Also, the death benefits vary and the liquidity features are not the same for each. Insurance companies that market annuities generally excel in one area or the other. After a consultation with an advisor one annuity may prove better for you than another but remember there is a give and take. Give up a little death benefit, gain a little living benefit and back and forth.

The Holy Grail for the investor looking for income is to be able to guarantee a lifelong income stream without giving up control or access to the asset. To be able to, in a sense, annuitize without annuitizing. There are various withdrawal features that flirt with this dream but never quite get there but some recent innovations seemed to have locked down the legal and financial issues that have in the past blocked access to the Holy Grail for annuity income.

A patented withdrawal method introduced by The Lincoln National Life Insurance Company has enabled income oriented investors to achieve what they haven't been able to achieve before. Lifetime income without loosing control of the asset.

I name Lincoln specifically because it is this innovative insurance company that has patented this withdrawal benefit and no one else in the industry has been able to use it. It is called *i4LIFE® Advantage*.

Please be sure that I have not in this book recommended one particular company over another. Nor am I suggesting this annuity is right for everyone. But for those seeking to create their own retirement income stream, retain access to their assets and the opportunity to have their income stream grow over time. This is absolutely one source of creating your retirement income stream that must be investigated before you make changes to your allocations or portfolios.

The *i4LIFE® Advantage* product feature addresses, as with other annuities, the main challenges individuals will face in retirement. Annuities as we have discussed, offer control and flexibility during the accumulation period. As your money grows, you have the option of changing the investment allocation. Pretty standard for most major variable annuity contracts. The guarantees for lifetime income are also available in different variations. It is the income side I am concerned about, not the death benefits, which makes this innovation so important for those seeking a lifelong income stream. Especially those that will need the opportunity to grow their income throughout their retirement years.

Without bogging you down with the nitty gritty details, the patented withdrawal feature in Lincoln's variable annuities works like this.

You invest a certain amount of money with the annuity company and based on your age, the length of time you would like the access for, and expected investment results, a current and minimum income level is set and you can view this prior to investing.

The real advantage for income seeking investors is that a large percentage of this withdrawal comes out tax free.

It works like this.

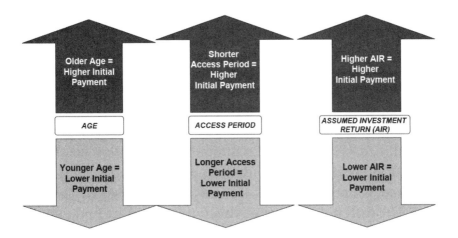

Source: The Lincoln National Life Insurance Company

Let's look at an example.

The *i4LIFE®* Advantage Payout
Portfolio Summary

Prepared For	Gender - Age	Start Date	State
Valued Client	Male 70	January 1, 1985	Pennsylvania

Purchase Payment	Cost Basis	Living Benefit Rider	Death Benefit
$1,000,000	$1,000,000	*i4LIFE®* Advantage Guaranteed Income Benefit	Guarantee of Principal

Initial Monthly *i4LIFE®* Income	Initial Monthly Guaranteed Income Benefit	Initial Monthly Non-taxable Income	Access Period
$5,612	$4,209	$4,218	15 Years

Investment Allocations
100% American Funds Insurance Series Growth-Income Fund

	Account Values					*i4LIFE®* Advantage with GIB			Death Benefit
						Lifetime Income Benefits			Elected Death Benefit
Age	Period Ending	Purchase Payments	Withdrawals	Account Value	Annual Returns	*i4LIFE®* Annual Income	Guaranteed Income Benefit	Non-taxable Income	Guarantee of Principal
				$1,000,000					$1,000,000
70	12/1985	$ 1,000,000	$0	$1,259,463	33.86%	$ 67,349	$ 50,511	$ 50,625	$1,259,463
71	12/1986	$0	$0	$1,410,658	19.66%	$87,339	$50,511	$50,625	$1,410,658
72	12/1987	$0	$0	$1,295,326	(1.06%)	$100,937	$50,511	$50,625	$1,295,326
73	12/1988	$0	$0	$1,345,664	11.75%	$95,857	$71,892	$50,625	$1,345,664
74	12/1989	$0	$153,421	$1,380,787	22.59%	$103,257	$71,892	$50,625	$1,380,787
75	12/1990	$0	$0	$1,201,589	(5.23%)	$110,182	$64,703	$50,625	$1,201,589
76	12/1991	$0	$0	$1,344,751	21.17%	$100,035	$75,026	$50,625	$1,344,751
77	12/1992	$0	$0	$1,293,513	5.15%	$117,235	$75,026	$50,625	$1,293,513
78	12/1993	$0	$0	$1,292,127	9.53%	$118,586	$75,026	$50,625	$1,292,127
79	12/1994	$0	$0	$1,161,905	(0.41%)	$125,174	$93,881	$50,625	$1,161,905
80	12/1995	$0	$0	$1,371,271	29.92%	$119,612	$93,881	$50,625	$1,371,271
81	12/1996	$0	$0	$1,423,924	15.77%	$151,005	$93,881	$50,625	$1,423,924
82	12/1997	$0	$0	$1,561,374	22.96%	$169,058	$126,794	$50,625	$1,561,374
83	12/1998	$0	$0	$1,582,288	15.31%	$201,779	$126,794	$50,625	$1,582,288
84	12/1999	$0	$0	$1,488,288	8.97%	$225,204	$126,794	$50,625	$1,488,288

Source: The Lincoln National Life Insurance Company

In this example we have a 70 year old male investing $1,000,000 in a Lincoln variable annuity. With the *i4LIFE®* *Advantage* the initial income level of $67,349 (6.7% of the initial deposit) is above the guaranteed amount of $50,511 (5.0% of the initial deposit). That initial income payment can fluctuate up and down depending on net investment return. In general, if your return is above 4%, your payment will rise, below 4% and your payment will drop but never below the guaranteed level. That guaranteed level can also be stepped up every three years if the investments have performed better than the 4% return, otherwise it will stay the same.

The difference between this type of annuity and others is that you have locked in a lifetime income stream, without giving up control or access to the asset and a large portion of which comes out **tax free** as long as you purchase it outside of a retirement account which is where this should be purchased. Out of the $67,349 income payment, $50,625 is not taxed at distribution (until the original cost basis is returned). For someone in a 35% tax bracket, that provides $61,495 (6.1% of the initial deposit) of income *after tax* the first year. If investment returns should drop the income level to the guaranteed amount, then the entire distribution comes out without tax. When you compare the after tax returns, *i4LIFE®* creates a much higher after tax level of income than other products and for those seeking income, that is the bottom line. ***What do I have left in my pocket after tax?*** A theme that we have been driving home chapter after chapter.

It also allows you access to the money and a death benefit which is not available if you annuitize as with other annuity contracts.

	Systematic Withdrawals	Annuitization Variable	Fixed	*i4LIFE®* Advantage
Flexible income (to combat inflation)	✓	✓	—	✓
Control of assets with death benefit	✓	—	—	✓
Lifetime income guarantee	—	✓	✓	✓
Investment control for market movements	✓	✓	—	✓

Source: The Lincoln National Life Insurance Company

As with all annuity contracts you need to examine the benefits and see if they are right for you. There are always positives and negatives with all contracts. If your intention is to guarantee your assets for your heirs using death benefit riders, the *i4LIFE® Advantage* may not be the best choice. There are other contracts that may accomplish this goal more efficiently. If you want make sure your principal is guaranteed to grow at a minimum certain rate, there are annuity contracts that will better accomplish this goal.

If your goal is to guarantee a lifetime source of income and to achieve the most tax efficient guaranteed annuity distribution available then this annuity, as my grandfather used to say, is the tops!

The patented *i4LIFE® Advantage* innovation for generating income is a great cash flow generation tool. Before finalizing other investment choices, see if the patented withdrawal benefit works in your families favor. It has, in my experience, created the best after tax cash flow for retirees than other products on the market.

Additional Death Benefit Rider

Investors are strongly advised to include this benefit in any type of annuity contract as it provides an additional level of protection for your beneficiaries beyond what we have already discussed.

Suppose, for example, you invest $100,000 in a variable annuity contract and, at the time of your death, the value has increased to $200,000. Under the guaranteed death benefit rider, your beneficiaries will receive $200,000.

However, if you had purchased the additional death benefit rider, they would also be entitled to an additional amount equal to a percentage of the annuities sub accounts earnings. In other words, your beneficiaries would also receive a percentage of the profits earned on the growth of your initial investment. That may be 40 percent or more depending on the insurance company.

Example E

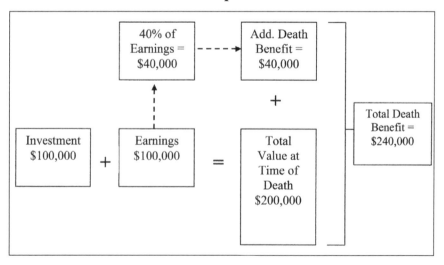

Chart 11
Source: AXA Equitable Life Accumulator
Variable Annuity

In the above example, your initial investment was $100,000 and the value of your annuity at the time of your death was $200,000. However, the investments of the contract produced a profit of $100,000. If, under the additional death benefits rider, your beneficiaries are entitled to 40 percent of the profit, then in addition to the $200,000 (the value of the annuity at the time of your death), they would receive $40,000 or 40 percent of the $100,000 profits. Thus, your beneficiaries would receive a total of $240,000. You can see why I strongly urge you to include this rider with your annuity contract. Example E.

When you begin investigating the possibility of purchasing an annuity, you are likely to hear a great deal about the similarities to mutual funds. The following table shows some of the benefits of annuities that are not available with mutual funds.

Annuities versus Mutual Funds

Having sung the praises of annuities for the last several paragraphs, it would be irresponsible not to point out that the advantages of annuities are not free. The fees, especially if one includes any one or all of the riders described, are higher than the fees on mutual funds. Whereas the fee for the average mutual fund would be around 1 percent of your total portfolio, the fee for the average annuity could be 2 or 3 percent—perhaps even a bit more, depending on the terms of the contract.

Again and again and again, it comes down to looking at your personal financial situation and doing your homework. Compare the advantages and disadvantages of annuities and mutual funds and decide if the additional cost of annuities is worth the added benefits. Ask yourself if the promise of safety, security, and ultimate peace of mind is worth the extra cost. For many investors (especially retirees), I have found, it is.

	Annuities	Mutual Funds
Rise when markets go up?	Yes	Yes
Decline when markets decline?	Yes	Yes
Have liquidity features?	Yes	Yes
Guarantee a rate of return?	Yes	No
Guarantee a death benefit?	Yes	No
Guarantee lifetime income?	Yes	No
Have an insurance benefit?	Yes	No
Help insure your retirement?	Yes	No
Protect your heirs?	Yes	No
Provide tax-deferred growth?	Yes	No

Chart 12
Source: Live Long Live Rich

Conclusion

To paraphrase the French author Blaise Pascal, for reasons that reason knoweth not, annuities often receive a great deal of bad press. Ominous headlines abound.

"Commissions of 10 percent." (<u>Fact</u>: Fees for annuities are usually nowhere near this high.)

"Never get out without a penalty." (<u>Fact</u>: In some annuity contracts, penalties expire in as little as one year. In most contracts, penalties expire in seven years or fewer.

"It's too expensive." (<u>Fact</u>: Yes. Annuities are more expensive than some other types of investments. Insurance companies indeed do charge for all those guarantees you receive. But when you consider the *value* of those guarantees and that you are unlikely to receive such guarantees—even for a price—with other types of investments, you may decide that the additional expense is a small price to pay.)

<u>Bottom line:</u> **Many investors will find annuities appealing as part of their retirement planning and income strategy because of the:**

- Potential to grow their money faster through tax deferral,
- Opportunity to more efficiently manage their retirement income,
- Death benefit protection riders for beneficiaries,
- Access to their money during retirement through a variety of payout options.

Annuities should be part of your retirement income strategy because they offer tax-deferred growth and potential significant long-term benefits. The tax benefits of deferred annuities can be substantial and the option of a guaranteed income stream is a thing devoutly to be wished.

<u>Do not buy an annuity without the help of a financial professional.</u> Annuities are complicated. Before making a purchase, consult an experienced financial advisor who can explain them to you.

Finally, <u>never purchase an annuity without thoroughly reviewing the prospectus of the insurance company.</u> Again, consult a financial professional for help. Purchasing an annuity is too important a decision to be made lightly or unadvisedly.

With those caveats in mind, annuities are a terrific way to help secure a happy retirement. Given the many available income options, you should be able to customize an annuity to fit your goals and risk preference.

Chapter 7

Investment Strategies

No doubt you have heard it said many times that men never want to stop and ask for directions, no matter how lost we are. Well, I am happy to count myself among the exceptions to that rule. Once during a family trip to a resort in New Mexico, I did get lost; and I was not the least bit hesitant about stopping to call the resort to ask for directions. Unfortunately, they needed to know where we were before they could tell me how to proceed. Even more unfortunately, I had no idea where we were, which made it hard for them to help me get us to our destination.

I mention this as a lead-in to a discussion of investment strategies, and to point out that, just as the resort people had trouble telling me how to get there when I did not know where I was, so too will you have trouble implementing an investment strategy without first knowing where you are, financially. In short, you cannot get where you want to go if you do not know where you are.

Unlike ordinary road maps, the financial road map's strategy changes constantly as our lives change and move forward. Therefore, the essence of financial planning is creating a *living financial program* that will change and shift in concert with your economic goals and needs, which will change over time.

To help you choose the right strategy, a financial calculator software CD is included with this book. To determine your current economic situation, begin by entering your financial data. The goal is to create a picture—in living black and white—of your financial future. For some this may not be (for the moment, at least) a pretty picture. However, it will help you identify and focus on accomplishing your goals and making tough choices.

Once you know where you stand financially, you can assess your current investments and asset allocation and decide if they will help you achieve your goals. A word of caution: Put aside all thoughts about past investment decisions—good or bad, i.e., what you bought, how much you bought it for, and how much it is selling for today. This is not an exercise you can do with your fingers crossed. This is about taking a hard look at your financial picture and making possibly difficult decisions about portfolio's investments and how they may need to be changed if you are to meet your financial goals, which include making your money last (preferably longer than you do), increasing your cash flow, and protecting your principal investment.

There are an infinite number of asset allocation possibilities. They may help you achieve the necessary diversification *with the proper amount of risk,* while at the same time increasing your income. On the following pages, I have provided a number of investment models. Remember: These are **_only guidelines_** to help you identify the right asset allocation based on the goals—and the risks—that are right for you and your family.

Illustration 1

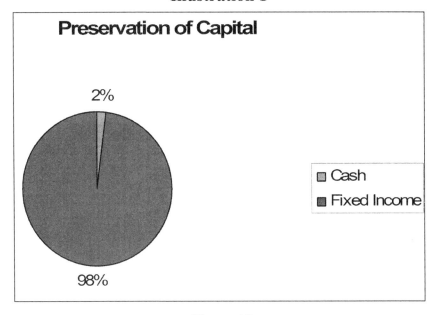

Chart 13
Source: Live Long Live Rich

Illustration 2

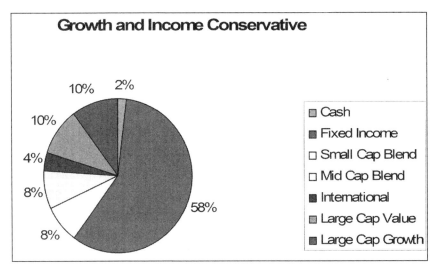

Chart 14
Source: Live Long Live Rich

Illustration 3

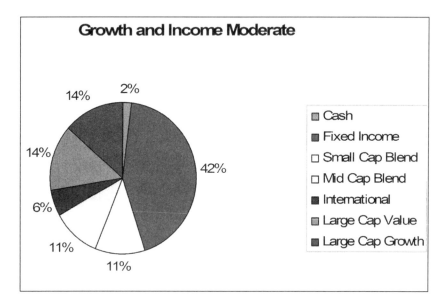

Chart 15
Source: Live Long Live Rich

Comparing the different models, you will notice that, as growth becomes more of a factor, the amount of stocks in the portfolio increases and the amount of bonds decreases. The more stock you have, the more volatile your portfolio will be.

The least aggressive of these models is the income portfolio (illustration 1), which has the largest amount of fixed income (i.e., bonds) 98 percent. By comparison. only 42 percent of the moderate growth and income portfolio (illustration 3) is dedicated to fixed income.

From an overall asset allocation perspective, it would be best to decide in advance what type of approach you are most comfortable. It may be that the advisor you have chosen uses the same or a different approach. If you trust the advisor (and why would you select an advisor you did not trust?), you may choose to use the strategy and process with which he/she is most familiar and comfortable. **Note:** Make sure you understand what the strategy is, how it will be implemented, and how it will be monitored before executing any of the transactions to implement the suggested plan.

Execution

After you have selected the portfolio that is right for you, the next step is determining how you want to arrange—or rearrange—the contents to fit within (or come close to) a particular model. For purposes of this discussion (and for the rest of this chapter), I will use the conservative growth and income portfolio (Illustration 2) as the basis for a *hypothetical* financial plan of action. In this hypothetical plan of action, I will use mostly mutual funds as the investment vehicle, so that I do not have to make day-to-day decisions about my portfolio. Example A shows how a portfolio might look, again, based on the conservative growth and income model and using mutual funds as the investment vehicle.

Note: All of the examples used in this book represent hypothetical situations only.

Example A

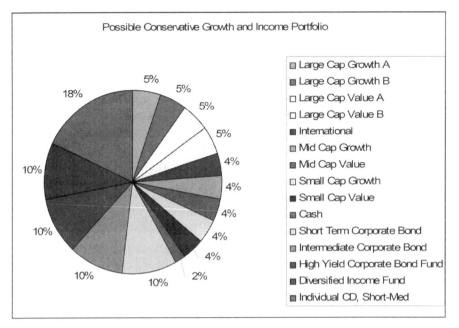

Chart 16
Provided by: Live Long Live Rich

Notice that instead of picking just one growth fund, I spread my investment between two different funds (and, by extension, two different fund managers.) In this way, if one fund manager is not having a good year, the other may provide the balance that I need to maintain my targeted returns.

Notice also that instead of buying a mid-cap and small cap blend fund, I decided to purchase individual parts—investing in one growth manager and one value manager for each. There is no right or wrong approach. This is just an example of a different way to "skin the cat."

On the fixed-income (bond) side, I chose corporate bond funds and spread that among different maturity levels. To keep a portion of my money safer, I added some certificates of deposit (CDs) to the mix, again, spreading out (or laddering) the investment from short to medium maturities. (I will discuss laddering in greater detail later in this chapter.)

Example B shows a different asset combination.

Example B

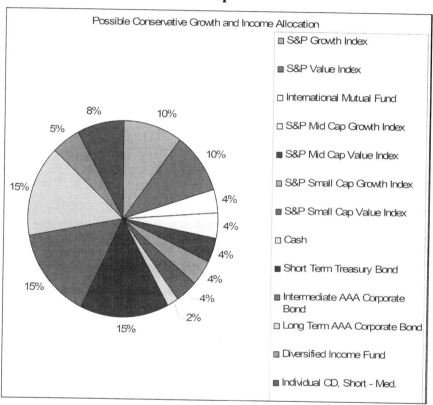

Chart 17
Provided by Live Long Live Rich

Here, I used primarily indices for my equity allocations. This combination, overall, mimics the overall market allowing asset allocation to determine your return. Note that I also included one international fund. Again, there is no right or wrong way to combine assets. You do not have to go all one way or the other. Arrange your assets in any way that works for you.

To make sure that the money matured, and that I received my principal back, I did not include any bond funds. Instead, I purchased a series of treasuries and AAA corporate bonds for safety—careful to stay at the *high end* of safety, as indicated by the AAA rating.

I chose a diversified income fund (which, perhaps, I read about in the business section of my local paper) because I wanted to include a variety of different fixed-income investments and because I was not comfortable making purchases of more complicated financial instruments on my own.

With the remaining cash, I laddered CDs that fit between the maturities of the corporate bonds. In this way, I will have money coming due every year to roll over if rates rise.

If you are wondering which example is better—A or B— the answer is neither. Each approach accomplishes the same thing just using different investments. One approach may do better one year and the other may outperform the following year. The basic principle remains: **Asset allocation determines how well a portfolio performs**. Keeping this in mind, you can participate in the markets in any way that works best for you.

Bond Strategies

Since trading bonds is not an issue for most investors (i.e., they simply buy bonds and hold them to maturity), the focus here is on ways to maximize income and protect your portfolio against the risks associated with bond investing. By keeping it simple, you may give up a bit in terms of interest earned, but your portfolio will remain under control and easy to manage.

The three top goals of bond investors are preserving principal, earning income, and managing tax liabilities.

Just as diversification helps to provide overall protection for your portfolio, so too does it provide protection when you are formulating a strategy for bond investing. Once you have determined how much to allocate to bonds, then you must decide where to place the funds, within each sector. For most investors the buy and hold strategy works. Not only do you know what your interest income will be, but you also know when you will get your principal back. This makes the bond portfolio straightforward and easy to manage.

Let us start with a few general rules.

With corporate bonds:

1. Invest in securities from different companies. That way if one company runs into trouble, hopefully your other investments will remain stable.
2. Invest across industry groups to further diversify your holdings.
3. Invest in different maturities to help limit interest rate risk and volatility.
4. Remember that old adage about not putting all your eggs in one basket? Well, that is particularly applicable when it comes to corporate bonds as the stunned employees of Enron and WorldCom (just to name two of the most infamous companies) will certainly now attest. In fact, there is a corollary to that old adage: If you must put all your eggs in one basket, watch that basket!

With government bonds:

1. Invest in different types such as agency, municipal, etc. This helps protect you against possible market fluctuations in any one sector.
2. As with corporate bonds, invest in different maturities to limit interest rate risk and volatility.

Bond Market Truths

1. When interest rates go up, bond prices decline. Conversely, when interest rates go down, bond prices rise. (Remember Happy Harry in chapter 3?) The tendency sometimes is to (perhaps unjustly) blame the advisor or, worse, to take an ostrich attitude (i.e., head in the sand) and assume that this could not happen to you. In fact, the relationship in principal value versus interest rates is mathematical. There is no need to assign blame to yourself or anyone else. To paraphrase retired CBS News anchor Walter Cronkite, "That's just the way it is."
2. Interest rates on long-term bonds are generally higher than on shorter-term bonds—something to remember if your goal is to maximize income.
3. Corporate bonds usually have higher rates than government bonds or CDs.
4. If an investment (bond or any other option) sounds too good to be true, it usually is not—good or true. So if someone tries to interest you in buying a bond (or any other type of investment) by guaranteeing that you absolutely cannot lose, be skeptical. You never get something for nothing, particularly not on Wall Street.

Execution and Laddering

The longer the maturity on a bond, the higher the interest rate you will receive. This is true across all segments of the bond market. If you are not sure about how long to invest, laddering the bond maturities in your portfolio is an excellent way to minimize risk. Laddering is the most popular strategy among bond investors, and it is particularly good for retirees.

Laddering is simply investing in bonds that mature year after year. For example, instead of buying all one-year CDs or all ten-year CDs, you might buy a *one-through-ten-year* CD ladder. Thus, if you were investing $100,000, you would be putting $10,000 into each year. (This is illustrated in example 1 on the next page.)

Laddering Example 1

Year/Maturity	Rate	$ Amount
1	2%	$10,000
2	2.5%	$10,000
3	3%	$10,000
4	3.5%	$10,000
5	4%	$10,000
6	4.5%	$10,000
7	5%	$10,000
8	5.5%	$10,000
9	6%	$10,000
10	6.5%	$10,000
Average 5	4.25%	$100,000

Source: Live Long Live Rich

In example 1, you have money coming due every year, and the overall average interest rate is better than it would be if you were to buy short-term bonds. When year 1 matures, roll it over (i.e., reinvest it) into the next unallocated year, in this case year 11, and so on. Example 2. In this way, your portfolio will move gradually, rather than dramatically, as rates change.

Example 2

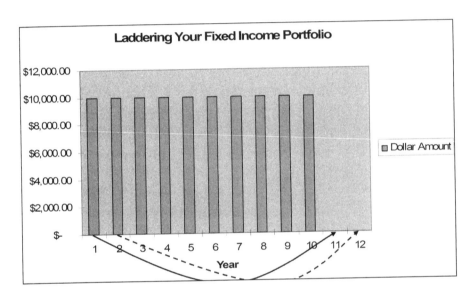

Chart 18
Source: Live Long Live Rich

If you put all your money into the ten-year CD, you would receive the maximum amount of interest; but you would also limit your ability to invest in CDs that pay higher rates should those rates rise over time. Additionally, should rates drop, you have locked in higher rates with a portion of your funds in the longer-term CDs. Laddering is a very effective way to limit the risks associated with interest rate fluctuations and market volatility.

On paper, we build a portfolio of bonds using CDs and Treasuries—the safest possible securities. Therefore, this is our benchmark. We can use the previous CD ladder example as a starting point. (See example 1.) The overall yield on this conservative laddered portfolio is 4.25 percent.

Now let us look at other sectors of the bond market to see what kind of risk I would have to take and if I can increase my interest earnings.

For example, I notice that one-year CD is paying 2 percent interest while a one-year AAA-rated corporate bond is paying 3 percent. Although AAA corporate bonds are not FDIC insured, they are a top quality investment. Question: Should I give up the FDIC insurance that comes with my one-year CD that is paying 2 percent in favor of the AAA corporate bond that is paying 3 percent? In most cases, the answer would be yes. Although AAA corporate bonds are not as safe as FDIC-insured CDs, they are considered top investment grade. Therefore, I would make that swap.

I also notice that a low-rated BB (i.e., below investment grade) bond with a one-year maturity is paying 4 percent. Question: Should I make another swap to get the extra 1 percent interest? In this case, the answer is no. My mother always told me there is a big difference between want and need. Therefore, if you do not need the additional income, it is generally not worth the additional risk. As a rule, you do not want to own below investment grade bonds. **<u>Remember:</u> Just one misstep in the bond market can wipe out years of income.**

As you build a portfolio, you will find that in some instances corporate bonds are paying more and other types of bonds are paying less, and vice versa. The market fluctuates constantly, so there is really no right way to tell you how much you should invest in which type of fixed-income security. Just remember to keep your risk in check and ladder your portfolio. With these things in mind, your investments should be comparatively stable and ready to pass on to your grandchildren when the time comes.

Using Bond Mutual Funds

Bond mutual funds—good idea or bad? Over the lifetime of your investments, you will see many different interest rate cycles. If interest rates go down, the bond mutual fund will look great. If interest rates are rising, it will probably look terrible. (Remember Happy Harry again.) Timing—and when you may need to sell some of your fund—will determine whether things have worked out for the best. Basic rule: Selling during a time of rising interest rates is bad. Selling at a time of falling rates is good.

Buying a high quality bond fund is comparatively easy both to understand and to do. Here are some things to consider before making a decision to invest in a bond mutual fund.

- Is the bond fund providing a better interest rate than you can get on an individual bond? If so, how?
- In buying and selling bonds, is the bond fund likely to provide you not only with higher interest earned but also with a better overall total return?
- Has the bond manager kept credit quality in check or has he or she been dipping into lower credit issues to boost the yield? In other words, is the bond fund manager's performance sufficient to warrant forgoing the promise of the return of principal upon maturity? Remember: Mutual funds make no such promise.

Although the literature provided by the bond fund you are considering will answer these questions, it is prudent to ask your financial advisor or fund company how the fund will react if there is an economic downturn or if interest rates are rising. These are issues where you need to formulate a solid, fact-based opinion prior to making a purchase.

Once you feel you have quantified the risks, then you can determine whether adding a professional manager to handle your bond portfolio, or some portion of it, makes sense for you.

To help you make the best possible choice here are two **hypothetical** examples.

Fund A: Average credit quality BB
Average maturity 10 years
Current interest rate 6 percent

Fund B: Average credit quality AA
Average maturity 5 years
Current interest Rate 5.25 percent

Which fund is better?

Based on the limited amount of information we have, I would argue that B is the better choice. The credit quality for Fund B is higher, and the average maturity is shorter. Although the interest rate is less, I would not feel that an additional .75 percent yield (as offered by Fund A) is worth the inherent risk that comes with buying a below investment grade rated bond.

Now let us make it a little more interesting. Suppose you learned that the manager for Fund A had been managing a portfolio of risky bonds for twenty years and has established an excellent track record, whereas the manager for Fund B has a mediocre record with only two years of experience. Which fund would you choose now—A or B? Well, before making a decision, you would need to weigh a number of other factors including the current interest rate trends and the economic environment. Are they up, down, or steady? How old is the manager for Fund A? Is he nearing retirement age? Looking at my current asset allocation, do I need some high-yield bonds to increase the level of diversification? These and other questions more germane to an individual portfolio should be answered before making a choice. The point is the interest rate is not the only factor to be considered in making investment decisions. Investors who consistently chase the highest interest rates usually run into trouble.

Now, let us add another investment possibility to the mix. In addition to Funds A and B, there is

Investment C: An individual corporate bond
Rating AA
Maturity 7 years
Interest rate 5.5%

Here we see high credit quality, an interest rate between those offered by Fund A and Fund B, and a maturity between A and B, but still with the additional promise that our principal will be returned regardless of where interest rates go. Would I choose the bond over the funds? All things being equal—yes. The *promise* by the company issuing the individual bond to pay back my principle at some point in time is very powerful. The credit rating is good, and the maturities and yields are comparatively close to fund A and B. Therefore, I would opt for the additional safety of the individual bond with the fixed maturity.

Let us add one more choice (and *assume* I am in a high tax bracket).

Investment D: A tax-free municipal bond
RatingAA
Maturity 7 years
Interest rate before tax 4.3 percent
Taxable equivalent yield 6 percent

By George, I think we've got it! Choice D offers a high credit rating, a fixed maturity, and a tax-free rate that, when factored in, is equivalent to a 6 percent taxable yield, the same as on the riskier bond investment. Therefore, D is a clear winner.

This exercise is designed to give you an idea of how you should be analyzing your options when trying to choose among fixed-income opportunities. Given this scenario, would it be wise to overweight a portfolio in municipal bonds? Yes, but remember that most of the situations you encounter will not be as clear-cut as what I have outlined here. Your decision, whatever it is, will come with a certain amount of risk. Your task before making that decision is to lessen the risk as much as possible. By fixing the maturity of your investments and avoiding riskier types of bonds, you would eliminate much of the risk. Suppose the high-yield bond sector does extremely well over the next five years. Then you would have missed an opportunity to make a considerable profit. Of course, you could overweight your portfolio with municipals (by a small amount) and underweight the other choices to maintain a balance. Again, diversification is the key in a bond portfolio (or any other kind). Whatever your decision, remember: betting "the ranch" on any **one** sector is a dangerous proposition fraught with risk.

Mutual Funds

If you have investments in income-producing mutual funds, then receiving the income is simple. Just call your advisor or Mutual Fund Company and ask them to send it to you. That is all there is to it.

What if your mutual fund is growth oriented and, therefore, does not produce income, per se? You could periodically call and liquidate a portion of your investment and have a check sent to you or you could set up a systematic withdrawal plan (SWP) to automate your withdrawals.

Systematic Withdrawal Plan

An SWP is an easy way to establish an income stream from your mutual fund holdings. It is a way to instruct your mutual fund company to sell a certain percentage or dollar amount of your investment periodically (monthly, quarterly, etc.) and send the proceeds to you or have the proceeds wired directly to your bank account. The fund company will continue to execute this transaction until you tell them to stop. You can establish regular payments from one or all of your funds. This is a flexible way to control your budget and the rate at which you liquidate your assets.

A word of caution: Make sure the amount you are taking out can be supported by the investment itself. A withdrawal rate of 20 percent, for example, would require a fund to produce this type of return year in and year out; otherwise, your principal would be depleted. A more acceptable withdrawal rate is closer to 4 or 5 percent.

Stocks

Stocks are sexy. They are exciting and intriguing certainly more so than bonds or mutual funds. At this juncture in your financial life, is excitement and intrigue what you are looking for? Some risk is appropriate for most investment portfolios, as long as it is tactical and involves no more than 1 or 2 percent of your assets. It is important to be realistic. We would all love to receive 10 percent dividends regularly—and risk free. That is not possible, at least not without more risk than most investors are prepared to take. Remember: Managing your portfolio is about *risk and reward.*

There are many ways to successfully manage your portfolio keeping these two factors in mind. Here are a few basic things to remember:

1. I have said it before, but it cannot be overemphasized: If an investment sounds too good to be true, it probably is. You say you were at a cocktail party when you heard about an absolute can't-miss-Internet high flyer? Like the man said, "Fahgeddaboutit!" What somebody else did with their money is not your concern—whether they made a fortune or lost one. Your only concern is your own money and how to make it work best for you. I can tell you from experience, 99.9 percent of the time, your best bet is to ignore rumors—no matter how good they sound or how well you think you know the source. If you would not gamble with your personal financial security and the security of your family at a roulette table, why do it based on nothing more than a hunch or something somebody said? If you get an uncontrollable itch to gamble, buy a lottery ticket. It is cheap; and when you lose (as you likely will), you will not have lost much.

2. Risk is okay but ***only*** with small amounts of money and ***only*** if you fully understand the nature of the risk.

3. The smartest and simplest way to control risk is through diversification. The right asset allocation will make the investment ride smoother, especially for individual portfolio management.

4. Don't be afraid to ask for help. Using a financial advisor does not mean that you abdicate your responsibility to educate yourself about your financial situation. The best advisors are experienced and

can act as a "sounding board" off which you can bounce ideas as they come to you and reduce your chances of making costly mistakes.

Choosing Sound Income Opportunities

First, make a list of your investments and how much you are earning from each one. (The software provided in this book will help you do this.)

After you have made your list, look at each investment and ask yourself: Do I like this holding? What is the potential? Is there another option that could provide me with a greater potential, or more safety (i.e., less risk)? A higher income stream?

My father-in-law loves golf. He plays often, and I like playing with him. I suppose I must have played with him fifty times; and every time as we approach the green, he asks, "What club do you think I should hit from here?" My response is always the same. "What club do you hit one hundred yards?" Of course, he has heard this before, and his face tells me he still does not know. I explain that he should take an afternoon and go out to the range, take out a club, and hit it ten times, marking down how far it goes. Then repeat the process for each club so that he will know exactly how far he should hit each club, assuming he hits it straight (which is a major assumption). Then, the next time he is on the course, he will know what club to hit.

Listing all your investments and analyzing each one allows you to see precisely which investments are performing well for you and which are not living up to your expectations. How do you go about identifying potential assets for sale"? Let us look at an example.

Suppose I own stock in the XYZ Company, and suppose that this stock has growth potential but pays no dividends (at least for the moment). Now let us say that I like this particular industry and want to remain invested in this market sector. Suppose one of XYZ's competitors, the ABC Corporation, is a larger, more established organization with less growth potential, but it pays a 3 percent dividend quarterly, whereas XYZ pays no dividends.

Question: Should I sell my stock in the XYZ Company and buy stock in the ABC Corporation in order to take advantage of ABC's dividend even though I would be giving up XYZ's growth potential? The answer is probably, but—there is usually a "but." The decision would have to be made based on an analysis of my entire portfolio to determine whether such a change in asset allocation would affect my overall investment objectives, and if so, in what way. Additionally, what are the *overall* prospects for ABC? Dividends are not the only factor.

Individual stocks can be risky and on occasion, may involve more risk than you are willing to take. In the situation outlined here, substituting a mutual fund or ETF for an individual stock may provide an increase in dividends, enhance diversification of the portfolio (always a good idea), and at the same time allow the investor to participate in any market sector. Small changes made over time can add up to a lot.

Bottom line? I am in no way suggesting that you should try to avoid all risk in your investment decisions. I am saying simply that you should manage your risk carefully in a way that protects your money and lets you sleep peacefully, which is worth a lot more than most—perhaps all—investments.

Monitoring Withdrawals

It is a peculiar characteristic of human nature that even people who have been very good about saving money during their working years often have no strategy in place when the time comes to withdraw that money—unless you call "take the money and run" a strategy. Of course, if your goal is to run out of money long before your retirement years are over, then "take the money and run" is, indeed, a strategy of sorts.

But seriously, folks. Before you start taking any withdrawals, make a list of all the assets on which you will depend for retirement income. Divide those assets into two categories: taxable and tax-deferred accounts. Next, decide whether you would like to receive your retirement income monthly, quarterly, or yearly.

Next, do your homework. There are two types of generally accepted withdrawal plans—dollar-adjusted and percentage. Neither is better or worse than the other is, and each has its advantages and disadvantages.

Under the *dollar-adjusted withdrawal plan*, you take out a certain amount and increase that amount each year by whatever the national rate of inflation happens to be at the time.

Using any one of a number of investment models with various combinations of returns, inflation rates, and allocation assets, you could determine, with a reasonable degree of certainty, how long these (hypothetical) assets would last under the dollar withdrawal plan. Using the software provided, you can customize a plan for your asset level and return expectations.

Advantages of the dollar-adjusted withdrawal include a reasonably predictable cash flow and the fact that the income is adjusted for inflation.

The *percentage withdrawal plan* allows you to withdraw the same percentage from your portfolio annually. Your income level will fluctuate each year because the value of your portfolio will change based on market fluctuations. Put another way, your income will be lower during unfavorable market periods and higher during favorable market periods. Percentage withdrawals are not adjusted for inflation. Rather, a long-term investment strategy is balanced in such a way as to cover that adjustment.

Advantages of the percentage withdrawal plan include:

- It is easier than the dollar-adjusted plan.
- Your assets are likely to last longer, given the fluctuations in income.
- During favorable market periods, your income might be high enough to allow you to withdraw the amount in excess of your needs or to leave that amount in the portfolio to take further advantage of future growth.

In an ideal world, you would be able to live quite comfortably throughout your retirement years off the interest from your retirement savings. Should you find it necessary to tap into your principal, however, proceed with great caution. Bear in mind also that you will need more each year to compensate for erosion caused by inflation. Using cash flow analysis and conservative assumptions should help you understand your limitations. Monitoring your withdrawals and maintaining flexibility in your spending habits will help you maintain a legitimate and workable withdrawal rate. The Live Long Live Rich software will help you monitor your balances and withdrawals and adjust accordingly.

Even if you are one of those who has put aside more than enough money to assure a comfortable—dare we say, lavish—retirement, it is still wise to pay close attention to withdrawals from your portfolio. If you have already formed the habit of monitoring your expenses against income, then you are ahead of the game. Be prepared to keep doing this during your retirement years. If you have not formed this habit, you must learn—preferably now.

Review your expenses against your portfolio holdings at least once a year to be sure that the asset mix you originally put in place is still working in your favor. Your income needs may change; and if that happens, you will need to reassess your asset allocation to ensure sufficient and continued income growth.

Withdrawals

The order in which you begin to draw down on your retirement savings will help to minimize the tax bite. <u>Rule of thumb:</u> Spend after-tax dollars first, followed by IRA dollars.

Since you are already paying taxes (on capital gains, dividends, and interest), make your first withdrawals from your taxable accounts.

The second target for withdrawals is IRAs, 401(k) plans, pensions, and any other retirement plans provided by your employer. Although these accounts should be allowed to grow for as long as possible, you are required by law to begin making minimum withdrawals when you reach 70 _.

As with all forms of advice, there is a catch to these suggested withdrawals patterns. If, for example, you have a good deal of money in an IRA or a 401(k), you might consider taking withdrawals before you reach 70 _. If you wait until the age of eligibility, even the required withdrawals may have the effect of putting you into a higher tax bracket. Thus a combination of withdrawals from IRAs and other taxable accounts before you reach 70 _ may help you to avoid the tax bracket increase. (See tactical withdrawals in chapter 2.)

Withdrawing money from 401(k) plans, etc., can be tricky. Be sure to explore all of the withdrawal options carefully before making any final decisions.

1. Some companies will allow you to convert your 401(k) savings into an annuity, which would guarantee you regular fixed payments in the future.

Advantage: A guaranteed income for the rest of your life or a certain period, without the challenge of managing your investments.
Disadvantage:There are many different types of annuities, and it can be difficult to separate a good policy from a poor one. Moreover, your employer's choices of annuities may be limited. For these reasons, you may wish to consider rolling the money in your 401(k) over into an IRA and then using the IRA funds to purchase an annuity. In this way, you can choose from a wider variety of annuities and options.

2. Some employers allow you to withdraw your 401(k) funds in installments over a specified number of years.

   Advantage: A steady stream of income without the rules that accompany an annuity.
   Disadvantage:You relinquish flexibility in handling your money, and your investment options are limited to those chosen by your employer.

3. Some companies will allow you to combine different options.

   Advantage: You can set up a plan that most closely suits your financial needs.
   Disadvantage: This option is often complicated and is likely to require a great deal of time, research, and planning.

4. Some companies will allow you to leave money in your 401(k) and withdraw it at a later date.

Advantages: If you do not need the money right away, this is an excellent way to maintain an already familiar investment.

Disadvantages: Your investment choices are limited to those selected by the plan administrator. In addition, should your company run into financial problems, perhaps leading to bankruptcy, there could be long delays before you got your money out or you could lose it all.

5. You could choose to take out your money in cash in a lump sum.

Advantage: Cash is always attractive and could be put to any number of uses, from buying a retirement home, to starting a business, to a plain old-fashioned spending spree.

Disadvantage: In the end, this could turn out to be the most expensive option. The funds will be subject to income tax and, under IRS regulations, your employer must withhold 20 percent of the lump sum toward that tax. If you are under 59 _, an additional 10 percent "early withdrawal penalty" will also apply. In general, this is not a good option to choose.

6. You may choose to roll over the lump sum of your 401(k) into a traditional IRA at a mutual fund company, bank, credit union, or other financial institution.

Advantage: Flexibility. You can invest IRA funds in stocks, bonds, mutual funds, CDs, or any other investment options you deem best for you. Moreover, you may sell them at any time.

Disadvantage: Rolling over your 401(k) may cause commissions, fees, and taxes to be assessed. <u>Note:</u> Among other things to consider, the rollover must be completed within sixty days of the withdrawal from your 401(k) plan. If you do not perform a direct custodian-to-custodian (i.e. firm-to-firm) transfer, the company may be required to withhold 20% of the distributions for taxes.

When you reach the age at which federally mandated minimum distributions from traditional IRAs and other retirement accounts becomes mandatory, by all means use those withdrawals first before tapping into any other accounts.

If you have not yet reached the age when minimum distributions become mandatory, your goal should be to make withdrawal choices that cause minimal disturbance in the asset allocation balance you have achieved and continue to maximize after-tax income. In short, make your withdrawals as tax-efficiently as possible.

At the same time, begin to identify assets among your taxable accounts that perhaps should be sold. *Selling* is not a four-letter word. Quite the contrary, it is a critical part of asset management, withdrawal, and continued investment income growth. Here are a few general rules to keep in mind when it comes to identifying saleable assets.

1. Taxable assets that have lost money could be sold. Use capital losses to offset capital gains and use the remaining amounts as deductions from ordinary income.
2. Taxable assets that you have held longer than a year should be considered for possible sale primarily because they are taxed at the long-term capital gains

rate. You may need to rebalance your portfolios asset allocation after the sales. Keep this in mind when choosing what to liquidate.

3. Consider retaining highly appreciated taxable assets with large capital gains. You might choose to pass these assets along to your heirs thus taking advantage of a stepped-up cost basis and to avoid capital gains tax for you.

4. Use company stock first to fund your retirement or to make charitable donations. Unlike inherited stock, on which your heirs would not have to pay a capital gains tax, stock in your company may have already received favorable treatment. If you have company stock, consult you accountant before making any decisions.

If I Had a Million Dollars

Ahhhhhh, if I had a million dollars what would I do with it? Let me lay out a (hypothetical) scenario.

Jim and Mary have been married over thirty years. They have two children, a boy and a girl. Each is married with families. Although each is in good shape financially, the Smiths would like to pass along an inheritance if possible.

Jim is in fair health, and Mary's health is good. Jim is about to retire and has found a good financial advisor. The advisor has assessed the couple's risk tolerance as moderate to low and has concluded that a conservative growth and income portfolio would suit them best for now.

Jim has decided to roll over his retirement plan at work to his advisor's firm so that he can more easily track the investment gains and monitor the results and withdrawals. Thus, he has consolidated all his assets with his current financial advisor.

Upon a review of the financial program suggested by the advisor, Jim and Mary conclude, along with their advisor, that they would need income of approximately $45,000 to reach their goals.

Husband: Jim Smith	**65**
Wife: Mary Smith	**63**
Assets in IRA	**$500,000**
Assets in savings	**$500,000**
Two grown children	**No longer living at home**
Home mortgage paid off	
No debts	
Expenses	**$45,000 per year**
Income from SS	**$15,000**

The example on the following page shows yet another potential allocation, this time using a systematic withdrawal from mutual funds. Following the illustration is a table showing the potential income one might expect from this type of portfolio arrangement. I could have added bond funds, annuities, or separately managed accounts along with a variety of other options. To simplify matters here, I illustrated a commonly used strategy in terms of investment breakdown using their projected social security benefit of $15,000 per year, an inflation rate of 3 percent, and a total effective tax rate of 23.1 percent.

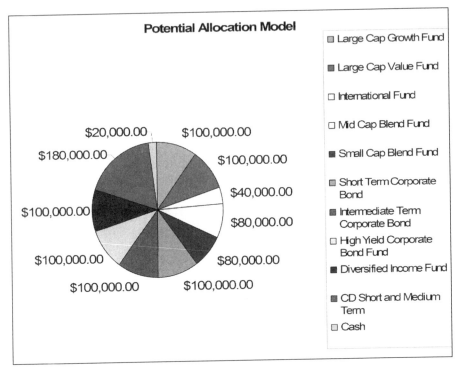

Potential Allocation Model

Legend:
- Large Cap Growth Fund
- Large Cap Value Fund
- International Fund
- Mid Cap Blend Fund
- Small Cap Blend Fund
- Short Term Corporate Bond
- Intermediate Term Corporate Bond
- High Yield Corporate Bond Fund
- Diversified Income Fund
- CD Short and Medium Term
- Cash

Pie chart values:
- $20,000.00
- $100,000.00
- $180,000.00
- $100,000.00
- $40,000.00
- $100,000.00
- $80,000.00
- $100,000.00
- $80,000.00
- $100,000.00
- $100,000.00

Chart 19
Provided by: Live Long Live Rich

Potential Income from the (above) Allocation Model				
$1,000,000 portfolio	Dollar Invested		Income	
Large Cap Growth 4% Systematic Withdrawal	$	100,000.00	$	4,000.00
Large Cap Value 4% Systematic Withdrawal	$	100,000.00	$	4,000.00
International Fund 4% Systematic Withdrawal	$	40,000.00	$	1,600.00
Mid Cap Blend Fund 4% Systematic Withdrawal	$	80,000.00	$	3,200.00
Small Cap Blend Fund 4% Systematic Withdrawal	$	80,000.00	$	3,200.00
Cash at 2.5% Interest	$	20,000.00	$	400.00
Short-Term Corporate Bond Avg. at 4%	$	00,000.00	$	4,000.00
Intermediate Term Corporate Bonds Avg. at 5%	$	100,000.00	$	5,000.00
High-Yield Corporate Bond Fund at 7%	$	100,000.00	$	7,000.00
Diversified Income Fund at 6%	$	100,000.00	$	6,000.00
CD Short- and Medium-Term Avg at 4.25	$	180,000.00	$	7,650.00
Total	$	1,000,000.00	$	**46,050.00**

Chart 20
Provided by: Live Long Live Rich

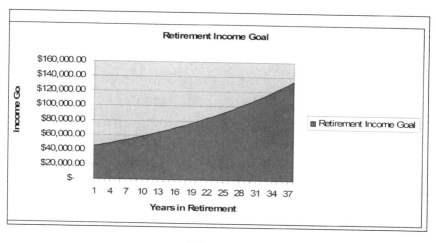

Chart 21
Provided by Torrid Technologies

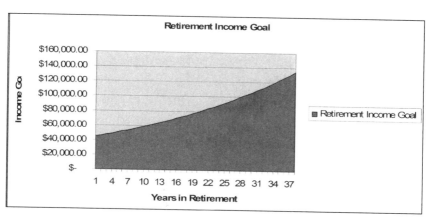

Chart 22
Provided by Torrid Technologies

As you can see, by setting up a diversified portfolio with an eye toward generating income, the Smiths were able to establish a portfolio that is properly allocated and income producing. Using basic withdrawal techniques, they were able to generate enough income to reach their goal. If you were to plug these numbers into your software, you will see that not only were they able to increase their income to keep pace with inflation but also achieve their secondary goal of leaving a nice little inheritance for their children.

As "Jim and Mary Smith" approach ninety years old, the value of their estate begins to drop. The longer you live, the more the chances of depleting your estate grow. That is why it is so important to monitor your withdrawals. If the Smiths remained in good health well into their golden years, they may have considered reducing their income stream to make sure their assets remained available.

It is all in the plan.

Ten Things to Do Now

1. Interview several financial advisors and, from that group, select the one with whom you feel most comfortable working, who understands your financial situation, and whose proposed plan of action you fully understand.
2. Consolidate accounts. You may have developed investment accounts with more than one or two firms. With the approach of retirement (or soon thereafter), however, it may be time to simplify and consolidate those accounts under one company. This will make assessing and managing your portfolio much easier and less time-consuming. Make sure the new firm has a Web site to check on your progress and statements that are easy to understand—for both *you and your spouse.*
3. Establish your risk tolerance using the questionnaire provided by your advisor.
4. Complete any financial planning paperwork to establish where you are today.
5. Estimate the amount of money you will need in the future.

6. Run a cash flow analysis to see if your current assets can sustain you through your retirement.
7. Select an asset allocation model.
8. Assess your current holdings to see if they fit into your new plan.
9. Execute the necessary transactions to realign your assets with your goals and financial needs.
10. Monitor your investments and withdrawals.

Chapter 8

Getting Help When You Need It

Do You Need It—Help That Is?

When it comes to human behavior, there is a long list of things that never seem to change. Among the top 10 is our deep reluctance to admit that we sometimes need help. The crazy thing about it is that this reluctance only comes into play when it concerns the areas of our lives that are most important. A Sunday afternoon duffer will move heaven and earth to get tips from some Tiger-Woods-wannabe on how to shave a few strokes off his game. Yet the same man often must be dragged kicking and screaming to the doctor for a checkup. He is quite likely to be equally reluctant to seek professional help if he is unsure about how to handle his retirement savings, i.e., about how to create an income stream that will last throughout his retirement years.

Fact: If you are unsure about how your retirement savings should be managed—if you are more willing to take advice from well-meaning friends and relatives than from an experienced professional then you are putting your retirement future at risk. There is an old saying: He who asks is a fool for five minutes, but he who does not ask remains a fool forever.

This chapter is about taking the "taboo" out of asking for help in handling your retirement savings.

Note: Nothing in this chapter should be construed as a recommendation of any individual, company, financial advisor, professional manager, or other financial expert. Our goal is simply to help you learn how to find the right people and to work with them in achieving the financial goals you have set for yourself and your family during your retirement years.

If you are successfully handling your retirement savings—if you have created the kind of retirement income stream that allows you to sleep peacefully every night, congratulations! You are in good shape.

Ask yourself this: What would happen if you could no longer handle your financial matters? Would your spouse know what to do? How will you and your family fair if there is a dramatic shift in your finances or if the economy suddenly swings one way or the other? From whom would you seek help?

Retirement is no longer the short-term proposition it once was. At some point, you will have questions (most retirees do) and you will need reliable help.

First, it is important to note that there is no one type of advisor or investment plan that is suitable for every one. All investors are different. Some prefer a more conservative approach. Others are more aggressive in their investment choices. Still others invest only when the moon is full and has moved into the seventh house of Venus. "Chacun à son gout." (Roughly translated, that is French for "Each to his own tastes.")

In this chapter, I have tried to cover the basics of selecting and working with a financial expert, including the different types of experts, types of investment accounts, and the fees charged for these services. I have also taken great pains to be as objective as possible since I am, after all, in "the business" myself.

Before we get into the different types of financial experts, let us talk about basic fee structures, i.e., how these experts are paid.

Fees

Financial professionals charge different fees depending on the type of service they provide. Make sure the fees are clearly spelled out so that you can decide whether you are comfortable with that particular fee structure. Some financial services professionals offer a variety of ways for clients to pay. Others may have only one fee structure. It is important to keep in mind that regardless of how the fee is to be paid, cost alone should never be the deciding factor as to whether you select a particular expert to assist you. A good financial advisor is worth his or her weight in gold as they can help you make your financial life run smoothly and profitably.

Now to basics. There are three types of fee structures used by financial professionals and financial management firms. Know also that advisors may be paid through a combination of these fee structures. For example, the planner may receive a fee *plus* a commission.

Standard Commission-Based Accounts

With this fee structure, you pay as you go for each transaction or product. The advisor is paid if you buy the financial products he or she suggests to implement his or her recommendations.

Right away, you can see the potential for a conflict of interest. How can you be sure that the product the advisor suggests is actually best for you in light of the fact that the advisor is only paid when you buy the product? In short, are they looking out for you or for themselves?

Although a few unscrupulous professionals have given this type of fee structure a bad name, the standard commission-based fee is not, by itself, a reason to take your business elsewhere. In fact, paying full commissions can be less expensive than a fee-based program.

For those investors who conduct only a few transactions a year and may therefore only need assistance periodically, the standard commissioned-based fee structure is likely to be the most cost effective.

Fee-Based Accounts

With a fee-based account, instead of paying for each individual transaction, the fee is calculated as a percentage of your total assets—usually 1 to 2 percent. Many investors prefer fee-based account structures for several reasons.

On the surface at least, it puts you and the advisor on the same side of the table—so to speak. What is in your best interest is in his or her best interest as well. Put another way, if your accounts assets grow, the advisor makes more money. Automatically his or her goals are aligned with yours. This is not to suggest that the advisor who is working on a standard commission-based account is not also trying to do what is best for you. The fee-based payment structure simply removes any doubt about the motives of the financial professional with whom you are working.

Fee-based accounts also provide other benefits. Many firms offer free retirement accounts to clients who agree to a fee-based payment structure. In addition, an array of no-load funds may be available for purchase—funds that are not available to the clients who pay regular commissions for professional financial services. Finally, under the fee-basedaccount structure there are no trading commissions (i.e., additional fees the advisor receives for each trade or transaction made). You pay for the trades through the annual fee, making this structure ideal for active traders who need the help of a professional advisor.

You should know that most brokerage firms offer both types of fee structures—standard commission-based and fee-based. If you are a new investor, it might be best to start with the standard commission-based fee until you have time to determine how many transactions you will be making per year. If it turns out that you have more transactions than you originally thought, any legitimate financial advisor will be happy to switch you over to a fee-based account.

Fee-for-Service

In this type of arrangement, advisors may charge an hourly rate, set a flat rate for a specific service, or receive a fee based on a percentage of assets or income. Planners who use this type of fee structure will rarely invest for you rather, they will tell you what they think you should do and you would have to execute the transactions on your own. Of course, the amount you pay the planner will depend on your needs. Even so, the planner should be prepared to provide an estimate of possible costs based on the services to be provided.

Now let us move on to what you need to know to find the right financial professional to help you.

Finding the Right Financial Professional

Clearly, what you want first in a money manager financial advisor is someone you can trust. *Trust*—a big word particularly in the financial services world. Trust is earned over time, yet most of us have an innate sense that tells us whether we can trust someone—a feeling that we have met a like personality, someone with whom we can get along. Use that sense. (Conversely, if some innate sense tells you that the financial professional with whom you are speaking cannot be trusted, use that sense too. Then use your feet to make a bee-line for the nearest exit.)

A successful relationship with a financial advisor grows over time to a point where you feel comfortable discussing your hopes and dreams and your concerns for yourself and your family's financial security. So while it may take time to find a financial advisor you can trust, it is time well spent; and once you find that person, do not let go. Let the relationship grow.

On a larger scale, selecting a professional money management firm can be complicated by a number of factors including mergers and consolidations that lead to unresponsive or impersonal service, high staff turnovers, lack of expertise, lack of comprehensive planning services, etc. Throw in the recent highly publicized securities and corporate scandals and you can see why the commodity in shortest supply may be trust! Remember, even if the firm you choose has a great reputation, it is your advisor who makes the decisions regarding your account. Make sure you are comfortable with that person or persons.

Ask about the services the firm provides. Financial services an advisors offer vary depending on credentials, registration, areas of expertise, and the overall organization of the firm. Some advisors offer financial advice on a range of topics but do not sell financial products (e.g., insurance, stocks, bonds, and mutual funds). Others may provide advice only in specific areas such as estate planning or taxation. Those who sell financial products and/or who give investment advice must be registered with state regulatory authorities and may have specialized certifications in their areas of expertise.

Ask about the financial advisor's approach—the process they prefer—particularly with regard to investment planning. Some prefer to develop detailed financial plans encompassing all of a client's financial goals. Others choose to work in specific areas such as taxation, estate planning, insurance, and investments. Ask whether the individual deals only with clients with a specific net worth and within a specific income level and whether the advisor will help you *implement* the plan he or she develops or refer you to others who will do so.

It is certainly not impossible to find reliable, experienced, trustworthy, competent financial assistance. You just have to be prepared to do your homework. When looking for a financial advisor, it is best to ask friends and relatives about their advisors and whether they are satisfied with the services they are receiving. A personal recommendation is often the best lead.

Now we get into the different types of financial experts, keeping in mind that, as with every other profession, some will always be better than others are.

Who's Who in Money Management?

There are professional money managers, financial planners, financial advisors, investment brokers, financial services professionals, etc. Small wonder how easy it is for you to get confused when you start looking for investment help. Just figuring out who does what—and for how much—is a challenge in itself.

To clear away some of the confusion, we have provided some basic definitions. Keep in mind that the lines between the various financial management professions do occasionally blur.

Retail Financial Advisor

Retail Financial advisors are also known as financial advisors, stockbrokers, financial consultants, and a few other titles. Whatever the title, these are financial experts who work for brokerage firms that employ them to handle customer accounts. These are also the financial professionals with whom most investors will be working.

In my career, I have worked with some excellent financial advisors. I have also worked with a few who, to be painfully honest, should have been wearing big red noses and floppy shoes. What you need to know is this: Although all financial advisors have to pass the same exams to receive their brokerage license, not all financial advisors *use* their knowledge in the same manner.

Retail investment firms offer a wide array of services and usually a full suite of investment professionals to help manage your planning needs and accounts.

Professional Money Manager

A professional money manager is hired to oversee and manage a portfolio. Money management firms are generally composed of individuals with expertise in different investment areas. With a professional money manager, investors receive minimal personalized service. It is more of a hands-off approach for investors. Usually the managers invest the assets and report quarterly on performance. You will initiate most contact when you have a question.

Certified Financial Planner (CFP®)

A certified financial planner has completed a course of study and a two-day comprehensive exam set out by the Certified Financial Planner Board of Standards, Inc. Study topics include, but are not limited to, investment, insurance, tax, estate and retirement planning. To receive certification, the planner must also demonstrate work experience and agree to abide by the code of ethics, professional responsibility, and financial planning standards set forth by the board.

A CFP practitioner can help you to understand your options in making the financial decisions that will facilitate achievement of your personal financial goals. Note: The CFP Board Web site provides information on the financial planning process and, most important, on current licensees. Thus, you can verify the certification of any planner before entrusting them with your personal financial information.

Certified Fund Specialist (CFS)

A certified fund specialist has completed training through the Institute of Business and Finance (IBF) and has demonstrated experience and expertise in mutual funds, annuities, and portfolio management. The CFS can help you select the best mutual fund for your investment. *If licensed to do so*, he or she can also buy and sell funds for clients.

Note: This designation is relatively easy to obtain and, for that reason, does not carry a lot of weight as far as I am concerned. Make sure the advisor has other training as well.

Certified Investment Management Analyst (CIMA)

The Investment Management Consultants Association grants this special designation only to those who have completed CIMA courses and who already have at least three years of experience as investment consultants. Those who hold this designation must be recertified every two years to prove their continuing expertise.

CIMAs usually work for financial consulting firms where extensive interaction with clients and management of large amounts of money are the norm. Those that hold this designation show a desire to continually educate themselves on the latest financial planning techniques.

Registered Investment Advisor (RIA)

This advisor is registered with the Securities and Exchange Commission (SEC). Under U.S. Law, RIA's owe their clients an ongoing fiduciary duty to provide full and complete disclosures of all fees and conflicts of interest. Additionally, they must demonstrate that all advice, purchases, fees and sales were appropriate, fair and clearly in the best interest of the client. The lines have blurred between stockbrokers and RIA's recently and the distinctions are part of an ongoing legal battle.

Chartered Financial Analyst (CFA)

This advisor has passed a test covering economics, accounting, security analysis, and money management. Testing is required for certification, so this is an excellent choice, among others, for your financial planning needs.

Accredited Wealth Management Advisor (AWMA)

A title earned by passing a comprehensive exam relating to all financial aspects an advisor may encounter when dealing with individual investors. This title is a sign that the advisor continues to educate him/herself and should be consider a sign of the advisors commitment to better serve his/her client base.

So—AWMA, CFP, CFS, CIMA, CFA—what does all this alphabet soup really mean? Well, if you are considering obtaining the services of a financial advisor, these certifications are a point in their favor, indicating that the person has put in many hours of study and, most important, has agreed to abide by a specific code of ethics and professional conduct. Although these designations are by no means the only criteria you should use in selecting a financial advisor, they do engender some measure of confidence in the expertise and experience of the individual.

Okay. Now you know what types of professional services are out there. It is time to get down to the nuts and bolts.

What Kind of Help Do You Need?

Before they know what they want to be advised about, many investors start looking for a financial advisor. So, first, decide exactly what kind of advice you are seeking. Perhaps all you want is someone who can give you an educated second opinion on a recent investment decision. If, however, you are looking for a firm or individual to provide you with ongoing long-term investment advice to help you achieve your financial goals, you will need to do some real research. This decision is too important to be treated lightly. Your aunt's brother-in-law may have worked for Merrill Lynch for thirty years, but that does not make him an expert on what *you* need to ensure *your* financial future.

So start by interviewing as many financial planners (or professional management firms) as possible to get good idea of what services are available.

Get detailed information on background, qualifications, and efforts to keep abreast of changes and developments in the field. Ask as many questions as you feel are necessary. Here are a few examples. You may think of others.

- What is your background?
- What is your process?
- Will you be handling my account personally?

- Will you be working with other professionals to develop a comprehensive program?
- What services do you offer?
- If I have a question, who would I call?

The best planners and money managers welcome questions as a sign of your knowledge and willingness to work closely with them. Do not forget to ask about certifications for those who will be working directly with you.

Pay particular attention to the level of experience of the person or firm. Ask how long the advisor has been in practice—always keeping in mind that a long track record does not mean much if the overall results have been less than successful.

Ask about experience in retirement planning, the number and types of firms with which he or she has been associated, and how that experience relates to the advisor's current practice. Ask about experience (or the experience of the firm) in dealing with retirees and other clients with financial situations similar to your own. Ask about specialized training.

Conflict of interest is an issue for financial advisors—and for you, as well, if you decide to use their services. An advisor, particularly one who is part of a money management firm, should have some degree of independence. As a client, you need assurance that the advisor's first priority will be helping you make financial gains—not ensuring profits for the company.

Of course, the advisor will need to ask you many questions as well—about your priorities, plans, family, etc. This information may be recorded, and you will probably be asked to sign a document verifying that the information you provided is correct.

The bottom line in finding the right financial help is this: Be prepared to do a lot of listening and observing before making any decisions. Pay close attention to any attempts by the advisor to steer the conversation in one direction or another. Your best interest should always be the center of the discussion. Does the person begin by asking questions or with an immediate sales pitch for company products and services?

Remember also that the final decision on who can provide you with the best financial assistance and advice must be based on what that person or firm can do for you—not on their name or location or the allure of office décor or a polished business card with raised lettering. In short, keep your eye on the doughnut—not on the hole!

Now that you have identified a few advisors to meet with, let us go over the process of deciding what to ask and what to expect.

Prior to meeting with an advisor, call to make an appointment and let him or her know why you are coming in. It will help the advisor prepare for the meeting and save time implementing the investment process.

The Process

Each advisor approaches a client differently and uses a different process to get achieve the client's investment goals.

Depending on the advisor's level of sophistication, which can vary from full-blown financial planning to planning on the back of a napkin, you can begin to determine which advisor is best for your particular needs.

I said it before, but this bears repeating: Pay close attention to any immediate attempts to steer the conversation toward products and services. Your best interest should be the main topic. The best advisors start by asking questions. Using the answers you provide, he or she can then begin to assess your situation with a view toward formulating and implementing (or helping you to implement) an investment plan.

For purposes of this book, we assume that you have some savings and at least the skeleton of a retirement plan in place. So based on your current situation, ask about the advisor's experience working with retirees and retirement planning. Ask also if the advisor will be working alone or with others (perhaps in his or her organization) to develop and implement financial recommendations. You have the right to meet everyone who will be handling your portfolio. Ask if the advisor would be willing to work closely with your accountant and/or lawyer if necessary.

Remember too that in selecting a financial advisor (or money management firm) you are establishing an important personal relationship. Find out if the advisor will be available to meet with you regularly or will meetings be limited to those times when some action is in order or something has happened that could affect your portfolio.

Here are a few other characteristics you will want to look for:

- The advisor should display a strong willingness to listen to, understand your financial goals, and provide you with a complete understanding of what actions they will take to help you reach those goals.
- The advisor should be willing to go over your current assets and formulate a coherent assessment of what you have in a way that you can understand.
- The advisor should be willing to take time—as much time as you need—to help you understand any and all information that pertains to your financial situation, the steps the advisor will take to help you achieve your financial goals, and how he or she will be paid for these services. An educated client is the best client. The best financial advisors know, understand, and appreciate that fact.

At this point, if you are satisfied with the answers you have received and the attitude the advisor has displayed and if you feel a synergy between your personalities, then you can begin to discuss in more detail your thoughts and dreams and the financial support you will need to fulfill those dreams. You can also divulge information about your current investments, savings accounts, etc., which the advisor will most likely want to look over so that he or she can provide you with an analysis of your financial situation.

The next stop is the actual formulation and implementation of a financial plan.

Financial Planning

A financial plan is the surest way to achieve your goals. Period. Even if you hit the lottery tomorrow, you would still need a financial plan to avoid ending up, as many lottery winners do, on the wrong end of a financial nightmare. Certainly, every investor should consider financial planning before moving into the more advanced stages of any investment process.

Financial planning worksheets, as provided by most firms, are an essential tool. Writing down everything that pertains to your finances and your needs—now and in the future—is critical. Without a detailed, comprehensive, all-inclusive accounting of where you are today, it is difficult, if not impossible, to formulate a plan that you and your advisor can use to help you chart a course for where you want to be, financially, in the future. Suffice to say, if the financial advisor you are considering does not strongly suggest that you complete a set of financial planning worksheets, find another advisor.

A full financial plan is the most detailed process of all. If after reviewing your financial situation the advisor recommends a full financial plan (as most advisors do), you must then decide for yourself whether it is worth the cost, which can be considerable.

Most full financial plans have several components, including but not limited to the following:

- An assessment of your current situation
- A reiteration of your goals
- An asset allocation analysis
- Recommendations
- Estate planning
- **A cash flow analysis**
- Whether you will achieve your goal

The first five items on this list are self-explanatory.

The highlighted point—the cash flow analysis—is the most important component for developing a retirement income stream. It is your way of finding out whether your assets will last long enough for you to achieve the goals you have set. The cash flow analysis is, in short, "the bottom line," or to use another analogy, "the sweet spot" of the retirement plan. It answers two tough questions:

1. How much do I need to earn on my current assets to ensure that I will have the exciting and fulfilling retirement that I have dreamed?
2. Do I need to lower my expectations?

Often in my discussions with clients, we go directly to the cash flow analysis.

Once you have calculated, in real numbers, the rate of return required and the percentage by which your assets need to grow and earn to support your goals, you have the magic numbers. Then you can ask your advisor to show you the plan he or she has devised to help you achieve these specific financial requirements and the risks involved if that plan fails.

Clearly, these are major issues that deserve comprehensive discussion.

Other Approaches

If it is determined that your financial situation does not require a full-blown financial plan, there are several other approaches. A partial or mini-financial plan, which may include nothing more than the cash flow analysis, may be sufficient. If you have selected the right financial advisor, he or she will know which approach is best for you.

At the very least, a good advisor will attempt to assess your investment risk tolerance by asking you a series of questions to determine if you have the stomach for riskier types of investments. In this way, it is easy to eliminate the types of investments with which you would not be comfortable.

Whatever the approach your advisor selects, make sure you fully understand the reasoning behind it, and what the advisor hopes to accomplish for you and your family's financial future.

We now come to the question of deciding what type of investment account is best for you.

Managed Money Accounts

Traditional Managed (or Separate) Accounts

For many, hiring a professional money manager is easy and gives them a sense of security that a real specialist is making their investment decisions for them. For this type of account, your advisor will have you fill out a questionnaire. Your answers will be used to determine whether you are a more aggressive or more conservative investor. The advisor will then divide your money between different independent managers who will handle different portions of your invest-ment.

Because these managers have contracts with the broker-age firms, minimum investment requirements, which can be in the millions of dollars, are waived. The brokerage firms monitor the performance of the managers each of whom is required to submit quarterly progress reports.

One of the biggest advantages of the traditional managed account is the comfort level it provides to the investors. You have no need to worry about which investments went up and which went down and how much you gained versus how much you may have lost and how to keep your portfolio bal-anced to compensate for these fluctuations. In a sense, you are managing your managers instead of the individual invest-ments—a much easier proposition and far more conducive to a good night's sleep.

Mutual Fund Wrap Accounts

Using the asset allocation process, you and your advisor may decide that the professional money management associ-ated with mutual funds may be best for you. With mutual fund wrap programs, you can buy a wide range of funds (including load and no load) that will help you reach your financial goals.

Mutual fund wrap accounts use the asset allocation process to rebalance your portfolio at specific intervals as determined by you and your advisor. Rebalancing may occur every quarter or once a year. Fees for the advisor, the trades, ongoing monitoring, and rebalancing are calculated as a per-centage of the total assets in your account—usually from _ to 1 percent.

In my experience, the regular fee-based accounts are preferable to mutual fund wrap accounts because they pro-vide you and your advisor with more flexibility in terms of investment choices, i.e., you are not limited to mutual funds; you can invest in other options as well. Having said that, however, many investors and their advisors find mutual fund wraps to be quite acceptable. You may too.

Exchange-Traded Fund (ETF) Wrap Accounts

ETF wraps are similar to mutual fund wraps but use exchange-traded funds instead of mutual funds as investment vehicles. More conservative, risk-averse investors are attracted to ETF wrap accounts because of the lower expense ratios compared to mutual fund wrap accounts. Asset allocation, usually derived through a questionnaire, is tweaked by the investment analysis and subsequent prediction of the firm. Suppose, for example, that you are a conservative investor who prefers to have only 10 percent of your portfolio in stocks. That 10 percent may be weighted toward (just as an example) utilities if the firm believes that utilities are the best investment at the time. This weighting will change often, as do the investment sectors in your account.

Conclusion

If you are looking for a financial advisor to help with your financial planning needs, you will find as many types as there are stars in the sky. Different fee structures and philosophies make it hard to choose. However, do not assume that all advisors are the same. Nothing could be further from the truth. Take your time. Keep looking until you find the advisor you have confidence in, and whose fees *and* approach to *your* financial needs are compatible with your vision of the best possible financial future for you and your family.

Brings us right back to where we started, doesn't it?

Chapter 9

Summary

We come to the end of this journey into the financial labyrinths of retirement. For you as retirees—recent or soon-to-be—it is only the beginning of what I hope will be many years of enjoying the lifestyle you dreamed of and which you worked so hard. We all know that there are no guarantees in life, but the right kind of financial cushion can certainly make all the difference.

To paraphrase disco diva Donna Summer, you worked hard for your money so you had better treat it right. That means understanding.

- That the old concept of retirement is gone—forever. Retirement in the twenty-first century begins with the challenges of a longer life span. Retire, in even reasonably good health, at sixty-five and you may live another twenty years or longer. (Did you know that the fastest growing segment of the population in this country is now people over the age of eighty-five?) With twenty or more years ahead of you *after* retirement, planning is not just a good idea anymore. It is critical—with a capital *C*.

- That planning ahead for retirement means making sound, fact-based decisions about what you want to do with those postretirement years and examining—in terms of real hard currency—whether you have created sufficient retirement income to allow you the freedom to do it. If you do not have a retirement plan, you need to get one started. *Now.*
- That diversification and asset allocation in your portfolio are the keys to optimum long-term performance of your investments and, therefore, to the income stream that will support your retirement. The portfolio models in chapter 7 are included as **guidelines** to help you identify the asset allocation that will work best for you, keeping in mind that the allocation will change over time depending on your financial needs and the vagaries of life, to which we are all subject.

With company-backed pension funds rapidly becoming outdated and fully funded Social Security benefits increasingly in doubt, focused and careful handling of IRAs, 401(k)s, and other retirement savings is more essential than ever before to your retirement future. "Take the money and run" may be a tempting retirement strategy, but it is not a smart one.

Rollovers, e.g., rolling funds from a 401(k) into an IRA, is often a good option, but even then you must do your homework, particularly with respect to IRS regulations governing these types of transactions, as well as RMD requirements. Suffice to say, this is one of those situations in which what you do not know *can* hurt you. A lot.

Chapter 2 provides basic information on retirement planning including strategies for handling IRAs, 401(k)s, and other savings. In addition to an IRA Distribution Calculation

Table, there is a discussion of the changes in tax laws and how they affect the types of investments that are best suited for IRAs and other retirement savings.

Chapters 3 and 4 covered the basic principles of investing in bonds and stocks. Because novice investors often find these topics a bit intimidating, I have attempted to explain the various types of securities and equities and the dos and don'ts of investing in them in a way that is easy to understand.

The best and most well diversified portfolios will hold some percentage of both bonds and stocks in addition to other investment options. How your portfolio is weighted (whether in favor of stocks or bonds) depends on where you are in your retirement years (early, middle, or latter years) and whether you are primarily interest in growing your portfolio or earning the most income from it or some combination of both.

Chapter 5 is an in-depth discussion of mutual funds, perhaps the most popular and easiest investment for the majority of retirees. Mutual fund companies make your life as an investor easy (or at least easier) by hiring managers to oversee the various styles of portfolios. A monthly (or sometimes quarterly) statement from the fund company gives you the value of your shares as well as periodic performance numbers. With the information, you can easily track the performance of the fund and your investment.

Mutual funds offer a number of attractions for investors. They are well regulated, which protects the investor from possible fraud. Mutual funds also provide the diversification that is critical to portfolio performance. This is a major benefit since most investors have neither the skill nor the time to constantly research and monitor portfolio investments and performance. Mutual funds invest in hundreds of individual securities thus ensuring that the failure of one investment within the fund will have little, if any effect, on the share price or on overall portfolio performance. There are fees associated with mutual funds, and some funds have minimum investment requirements. However, even taking these things into the consideration, mutual funds are still a comparatively inexpensive way to diversify.

Chapter 6 is a comprehensive discussion of annuities, which often get a bad rap in the press. Potential investors are warned away from annuities because of:

- The commissions, which are usually never as high as they are portrayed;
- The penalties that investors have to pay if they want to get their money out, even though in most annuity contracts the penalties expire in fewer than seven years;
- The fact that annuities are expensive, which is true, but when you consider the value of the guarantees that come with annuities, the additional expense may well be a small price to pay.

Even considering these issues, my personal view is that annuities are a great option for most investors. Benefits of annuities include the potential to grow your money faster through tax-deferrals and the opportunity to manage efficiently your retirement income. Death benefit riders, available (for a fee) with most annuities, are another attractive feature of this type of investment. Finally, there are varieties of payout options with annuities, some that carry fees that give investors reasonably ready access to their money. This is a particularly valuable in times of sudden financial crisis.

In short, annuities are an excellent means of helping to ensure a secure cushion for your retirement.

Chapter 7 is a nuts-and-bolts discussion of investment strategies. There are dozens of different options. My goal was to provide you with some very basic **guidelines** to help you choose the right financial strategy for your retirement. Using the financial calculator software CD included with this book, you can create a picture of your financial future starting with an analysis of your financial "present," i.e., where you stand right now. The idea is to assess your current investments and asset allocations, and by doing so, determine whether they will help you achieve your financial goals, or what steps to take if your current investments need to be rearranged, as may well be the case.

Finally, chapter 8 is about getting help when you need it. You may be surprised to learn that many people are more reluctant to ask for help in financial matters than in personal and/or health matters, even though an uncertain financial future will almost certainly have a negative effect on all other aspects of their lives.

Bottom line? Most, if not all, investors will need help from a financial advisor, planner, or other financial professional at some time. This is nothing for you to be ashamed. The trick is to be sure you do your homework to find the best and most reliable assistance. Before you open up the "diary" of your financial life to any financial professional, make sure that person has your interest in mind and that you understand the strategies and steps he or she proposes to take to help you reach your financial goals.

I will leave you with one last thought, something that I have said more than once in these pages, but cannot be stated too often: **There are no risk-free investments**. Do not believe anyone who tells you otherwise, regardless of how well you think you know them or how well meaning they seem.

You worked hard for your money. Treat it right.

Sources

American Association of Retired Persons (AARP), www.aarp.org/money/financial_planning

"Medical Costs II," by Glenn Ruffenach, Wall Street Journal, May 22, 2005

"Health Benefits Offered by Firms Shrink for Retirees," by Christopher Conkey, Wall Street Journal, March 23, 2005.

"The End of Retirement," speech by William D. Novelli, Executive Director and CEO, American Association of Retired Persons (AARP), Institute for Public Relations, November 15, 2001.

Employee Benefit Research Institute (EBRI) and Matthew Greenwald & Associates, Inc., Retirement Confidence Surveys (RCS), http://www.ebri.org/pdf/survey/rcs 2005.

American Savings Education Council (ASEC) 2003 Survey on Retirement Savings and Workers

"Unanticipated Retirement Expenses," The T. Rowe Price Investor, June 2005 (Based on information from "The Center for Retirement Research: Understanding Expenditure Patterns in Retirement," Boston College 2005, and "Kelley Blue Book.").

"Retirement Distributions: Creating a Limitless Income Stream for an 'Unknowable Longevity'" by Nancy Opiela, FOCUS, www.fpanet.org/journal/artcles/2004_issues

"Taking Distributions from your IRA," AARP Bulletin, August 14, 2002.

"Health Care in the 21st Century," speech by William D. Novelli, Executive Director and CEO, AARP, American College of Physicians (AC) dinner, Washington, DC May 21, 2002.

"Unanticipated Retirement Expenses," The T. Rowe Price Investor, June 2005 (Based on information from "The Center for Retirement Research: Understanding Expenditure Patterns in Retirement," Boston College 2005.

"The Big Retirement Headache," by Lisa Gibbs, Money Magazine, April 27, 2005.

"Retirement: It's Going to Cost You," by Sarah Max, CNN/Money Staff Writer, March 28, 2005.

"Retirees on Track for 59 percent of Income," by Kaja Whitehouse, DOW JONES NEWSWIRES COLUMN, June 7, 2005.

"You May Overestimate Retirement Needs," by Kaja Whitehouse, DOW JONES NEWSWIRES COLUMN, June 23, 2005.

"Retirement Planning: Survey Shows Growing Investor Demand for Retirement Advice," by Lingling Wei, DOW JONES NEWSWIRES, June 23, 2005.

"Burning Through Money in Retirement: A Tale of Three Withdrawal Strategies," by Jonathan Clements, Wall Street Journal, April 27, 2005.

"Take the Cash and Run? Or Should You Find A Better Way to Pull Money from your 401 (k) Account," by Ellen Hoffman, AARP Bulletin, July/August 2002.

"Hungry for Those T-Bills," The Monitor's View, Christian Science Monitor, May 9, 2005.

"What To Leave Behind: Choosing Assets that will Benefit Your Kids the Most," by Jonathan Clements

"The Retirement Race" by Jane Bryant Quinn, Temma Ehrenfeld, Ari Berman, Jason McLure, Ellise Pierce, Joan Raymond, and Lynn Waddell, Newsweek Magazine, March 2004

www.vanguard.com, Planning and Education, Vanguard Retirement Center, Plain Talk on Retirement Planning.

"Simplicity Has Its Rewards When Setting Portfolio," by John Waggoner, USA Today, July 8, 2005.

"A Wave of 401(k) Rollovers Builds: Workers Face Four Options on Finding Homes for Cash in Retirement-Savings Plans," by Kathy Chu, Wall Street Journal, February 1, 2005.

"Shifting Gears, and Funds, Into Equities," by Conrad de Aenlle, New York Times, June 25, 2005.

"How to Hedge Against Two Scary Scenarios," John Waggoner, USA Today, July 1, 2005.

"Stock Answers To Retirement Puzzles," Karen Damato, Wall Street Journal, May 13, 2005.

"Benefits and Drawbacks of Mutual Funds," www.aarp.org/money/financial_planning/investing_saving

"Creating a Retirement Paycheck," by Walter Updegrave, Ask The Expert, www.money.com. May 2004.

"The Basics of Bond Duration," Columbia Management

"Medigap Plans: Medicare Supplemental Insurance Policies," www.aarp.org/health. Search: Medigap.

"Retirement Distributions: Creating a Limitless Income Stream for an 'Unknowable Longevity'," by Nancy Opiela (Freelance writer in Medfield, Massachusetts and an associate editor of the *Journal of Financial Planning*.) www.fpanet.org/journal/articles/2004_issues

Google Search: Scudder Investments Open Web site. Scroll: Retirement Plans. Select Scudder University. Click on "learn more"

"Changes in Retirement" by Jack Piazza Sensible Investment Strategies, www.seninvest.com/article 8

www.investopedia.com/dictionary/articles, "The Uses and Limits of Volatility," by David Harper, Editor-in-Chief, Investopedia Advisor, February 18, 2004.

"Changes in Retirement" by Jack Piazza Sensible Investment Strategies, www.seninvest.com/article 8

"Smart Money Fund Screen/Funds for Retirees," by Joshua Albertson, Wall Street Journal, June 28, 2005.

www.vanguard.com, Planning and Education, Vanguard Retirement Center, Plain Talk on Retirement Planning.

"Diversifying Your Portfolio," The T. Rowe Price Investor, June 2005.

"Asset Allocation," The Bond Market Association, Investing in Bonds.com http://www.investinginbonds.com/learnmore.asp

"This Inflation Hedge Can Be a Bit Volatile," J. Alex Tarquinio, New York Times, July 10, 2005.

"Bank-Based Savings Instruments," www.aarp.org. Search: Money and Work

Google Search: Commodity + Definition: http://www.investopedia.com/terms

"Helping Boomers Chart Their Course," by Karen Damato, Wall Street Journal, June 6, 2005.

"Got Enough Saved for Retirement," by Kelly Greene, Wall Street Journal

"Help America Retire," "The American Retirement Revolution," www.hartfordinvestor.com

Live Long and Prosper: Invest in Your Happiness, Health, and Wealth for Retirement and Beyond by Steve Vernon, John Wiley & Sons, Inc., Hoboken, New Jersey, 2005.

"Retirees Go It Alone on 401(k) Rollovers," Wall Street Journal, March 1, 2005.

"How Retirees Are Blowing Their Nest Eggs," Kelly Green, Wall Street Journal (Atlanta), June 27, 2005.

"Pension Roulette: Millions of Americans are losing promised benefits. How Secure is your future?" by Tim Gray, AARP Bulletin, July/August 2005.

"Making Your Money Last Through Retirement," National Endowment for Financial Education, Google Search: AARP/Retirement/Article Title

"What You Should Know [about] the Risks of Investing in Bonds," the Bond Market Association, www.investinginbonds.com/learnmore

The Bond Market Foundation, www.bondmarkets.org.

Live It Up Without Outliving Your Money: 10 Steps to a Perfect Retirement Portfolio, by Paul Merriman, John Wiley & Sons, Inc., Hoboken, New Jersey, 2005.

"Looking Long Term? Get Your Glasses," Mark Hulbert, Editor, The Hulbert Financial Digest, MarketWatch, New York Times, June 19, 2005.

"How to Hedge Against Two Scary Scenarios," by John Waggoner, USA Today, July 1, 2005.

"An Overview of Annuities," by Chris Gallant, http://www.invesopedia.com/articles/retirement, June 30, 2005.

"Family Finance: Groups Push Annuities as a Way to Stretch a Retirement Nest Egg," by Jeff Opdyke, Wall Street Journal, September 8, 2004.

"Selecting the Payout on Your Annuity," by Steven Merkel, www.investopedia.com/articles/retirement, July 11, 2005.

"Adding Balance to Retirement," by Paul B. Brown, New York Times, April 10, 2005.

"You May Live Long, but Will You Prosper? Too Few Hold Realistic View of Financial Needs for Retirement," Sandra Block, USA Today, June 10, 2005.

"Advisors to Play Bigger Role in Sales: Retiring Baby Boomers Will More on Pros to Manage Complex Assets," by Arden Dale, Wall Street Journal, February 24, 2005.

Google Search: Mutual Fund—Definition, www.investorwords.com

"Adding Balance to Retirement," by Paul B. Brown, New York Times, April 10, 2005.

"What You Leave Behind: Choosing Assets That Will Benefit Your Kids the Most," from column "Getting Going" by Jonathan Clements, The Wall Street Journal,

Focus: Retirement Distributions: Creating a Limitless Income Stream for an 'Unknowable Longevity, by Nancy Opiela (Freelance writer in Medfield, Massachusetts, and an associate editor of the *Journal of Financial Planning*.) www.fpanet.org/journal/articles/2004_issues

"10 Questions You Should Ask Yourself Now About Retirement," Sandra, Block, John Waggoner, and Mindy Fetterman, USA Today, June 9, 2005.

"Introduction to Mutual Fund Wraps" by Jim McWhinney, www.investopedia.com/articles, May 3, 2005.

"The Alphabet Soup of Financial Certifications," by Investopedia staff, www.investopedia.com/articles, April 15, 2005.

Money Manager—Definition, www.investopedia.com/dictionary

Wrap Account—Definition, www.investopedia.com/dictionary

"Wrap It Up: The Vocabulary and Benefits of Managed Money," by Jim McWhinney, www.investopedia.com/articles, February 1, 2005.

"Choosing an Advisor: Wall Street vs. Main Street," by Jim McWhinney, www.investopedia.com/articles, June 9, 2005.

"Shopping for a Financial Advisor," by Investopedia staff, www.investopedia.com/articles, October 17, 2003.

"Which One Should You Listen To: Financial Advisors Can Have Conflicts of Interest, So Do a Little Digging," by Kathy Chu, USA Today, August 5, 2005.

"Wealth Manager: Wealthy Lose Trust in Advisors," by Rachel Emma Silverman, Wall Street Journal, February 2, 2005

"Financial Planners' Advice May Be Biased, Too," by Karen Damato, Wall Street Journal, June 17, 2005.

"Financial Planners Target Boomers: Some Advisors Set Focus On Challenges that Await Retirees and Their Families," Colleen DeBaise, Wall Street Journal, August 16, 2005.

"Introduction to Exchange-Traded Funds," Investopedia Staff, www.investopedia.com, April 1, 2005.

"Advantages of Exchange-Traded Funds," by Jim McWhinney, www.investopedia.com, June 6, 2005.

"Finding Money in Banks," by James K. Glassman, The Washington Post, February 1, 2004.

"Will Fame and Fortune Change Utility Stocks," Conrad deAenille, New York Times, July 31, 2005.

"Utility Stocks Climb On Impending New Law," Elliot Blair Smith, USA Today, August 2, 2005.

"Types of REITS," Investopedia Staff, www.investopedia.com

Metlife.com Annuities

Immediate Annuties.com

AXA Annuities

Wachovia Securities MLP Primer

ETFConnect.com

Research Magazine Guide to REITS.

MSN Money

PIMCO.com Bonds

Understanding Stocks and Bonds.com Bond Basics

InvestinginBonds.com

Torrid Technologies: www.torrid-tech.com

Additional Resources

General Information on Retirement

American Association of Retired Persons (AARP) (www.aarp.org.) Search word—retirement

American Savings Education Council (ASEC) (http://www.choosetosave.org/asec)

U.S. Department of Labor/Employee Retirement Income Security Act (www.dol.gov/dol/topic/retirement/erisa.htm)

Health Care Information

State Health Insurance Assistance Program (SHIP)—a free program that provides advice and counseling for older adults about health-related topics. For the nearest SHIP program, call Eldercare Locator at 1-800-677-1116.

Healthinsuranceinfo.net

Financial Information

Mutual Funds

The Alliance for Investor Education

http://www.investoreducation.org

This Web site includes a "Guide to Understanding Mutual Funds" as well as a fund fee calculator.

The Securities and Exchange Commission (SEC)

http://www.sec.gov

On the SEC Web site, you can find online publications about mutual funds, interactive tools, and a fund cost calculator to help you compare true dollar cost of different funds. Through the EDGAR Database (under SEC Filings and Forms"), you can also find and read various mutual fund prospectuses.

The Investment Company Institute (ICI)

http://www.ici.org

As trade organization for the mutual funds industry, the Investment Company Institute (ICI) Web site provides a great deal of information, including "A Guide to Understanding Mutual Funds" and "Mutual Fund Fact Book."

Federal Deposit Insurance Corporation (FDIC)

www.fdic.gov or publicinfo@fdic.gov

To contact the author:
www.LivelongLiverich.com